C000226184

# STALLONE! A HERO'S STORY

On the Final Day of Shooting for *Rocky III*,
During a Superhuman Swimming Routine,
Stallone Went into Shock ... trembling and
breathing rapidly, he struggled to reach the
side of the pool. Helped from the water, he
was stretched out on a towel, where his skin
went white and his body temperature
plummeted.

'My heart was doing 210 beats a minute,' he
says with a shiver, 'and the paramedics gave
me oxygen ... that was the only time in my life
that I was *really* frightened. My body seemed
to be saying, "I can't take it anymore, Stallone,
you've pushed me to the limit. I quit."'

But Stallone, being Stallone, didn't quit; if
anything, having his body revolt like that only
seemed to strengthen his resolve to make it do
what he wanted.

# Stallone!

## A Hero's Story

---

# Jeff Rovin

**NEW ENGLISH LIBRARY**
Hodder and Stoughton

Copyright © 1985 by Jeff Rovin

First published in the United States of America in 1985 by
Pocket Books

NEL Paperback edition 1987

**British Library C.I.P.**

Rovin, Jeff
   Stallone! a hero's story.
   1. Stallone, Sylvester   2. Moving-picture actors and
   actresses—United States—Biography
   I. Title
   791.43'028'0924      PN2287.S667

   ISBN 0-450-40938-4

Printed and bound in Great Britain for
Hodder and Stoughton Paperbacks, a
division of Hodder and Stoughton Ltd.,
Mill Road, Dunton Green, Sevenoaks,
Kent (Editorial Office: 47 Bedford
Square, London WC1B 3DP) by
Richard Clay Ltd., Bungay, Suffolk

# STALLONE!

# Prologue

The night of March 15, 1975, was a historic one for Sylvester Stallone. On that night, in a movie theater brightened by the light of a half-dozen projection televisions, Sylvester conceived of the character that would not only salvage his floundering career but would also become a contemporary legend.

For over five years, the hulking Stallone had scratched out a living as an actor and a writer. He'd played mostly muggers and losers, characters he describes as "one step away from the electric chair"; he'd gone nude on the stage and, in order to buy food, had even acted in a pornographic film. He'd also written a stack of screenplays and teleplays, though his percentage of sales was low.

Finally, on his twenty-ninth birthday, Sylvester had what he calls "a sudden revelation." Sitting with his wife in his small, dingy Los Angeles apartment, he decided that the only way to escape his dead-ended career was "to write the kind of screenplay that I personally enjoyed seeing," a story of "heroism, great love, dignity, and courage, of people rising above their stations, taking life by the throat and not letting go until they succeeded." And having written such a film, he would find a way to star in it as well. Sylvester was convinced that if he could come up with a project like that, someone somewhere in Hollywood might be persuaded to bring it to the screen.

First, of course, he had to find an appropriate subject.

Sylvester had been a student of people and of movies for a long time, and he realized that there were many kinds of stories to tell about heroism. He could write a western, a war film, a sports story, even a political drama along the lines of *Mr. Smith Goes to Washington*. He remembers, "I had so many ideas in my head I couldn't focus on any one."

On the night of March 15, he dipped into his savings—which had dwindled to a meager $106—and, to try and clear his head, bought himself a ticket to a closed-circuit TV broadcast of the Muhammad Ali–Chuck Wepner championship boxing match. A former boxing coach himself, Sylvester had always found championship bouts inspiring and hoped this one would help get his creative juices flowing.

As it happens, this particular fight was considered something of a farce by boxing pundits. Despite the fact that a title was at stake, Wepner wasn't considered a top contender; in fact, he was known, rather unflatteringly, as "the Bayonne Bleeder." Wepner was simply someone on whom Ali could practice without seriously jeopardizing his title.

To Wepner, of course, the fight was anything but a joke. The challenger realized that this was his one shot at the top, and he worked hard to get into peak physical shape. He also told anyone who would listen that regardless of what the experts were saying, the Greatest would not be mopping the floor with him. No one believed the challenger, but his words proved prophetic; on the night of the fight, Ali had his hands full. Wepner lasted the entire fifteen rounds and at one point even knocked the monolithic Ali to the canvas. While the challenger did not come away with the title, he was definitely a champion that night.

Sitting in the theater, Sylvester was deeply impressed by Wepner's courage and determination. "They said he couldn't last three rounds," the actor recalls, "but as the fight progressed this miracle unfolded. He hung in there and people went absolutely crazy. We had witnessed an incredible triumph of the human spirit and we loved it." Sylvester left the theater preoccupied with the image of this man who refused to go down, and, as he says, "that night, Rocky Balboa was born."

Needless to say, Rocky Balboa would end the poverty and anonymity that had plagued Sylvester Stallone, though at the same time he introduced a whole new set of problems. Fame, he would learn the hard way, can be more troublesome, debilitating, and downright dangerous than hunger and the leanest of years.

Fortunately, Sylvester is one of the film industry's most resilient figures. Unlike his legendary screen heroes, Rocky and Rambo, he doesn't triumph by balling his fists or shouldering an AR-15 rifle. His weapons are intelligence, innate confidence, an all-important sense of humor, and a generous helping of poise—qualities that have not only helped him to survive but make Sylvester's story in many ways more compelling and heroic than those of his fictional characters.

# Chapter

## One

The long, strenuous climb of Sylvester Stallone—what he calls a "roaches to riches" story—began, appropriately enough, in the section of New York City informally known as Hell's Kitchen. Lying west of the Times Square theater district, stretching from 9th Avenue to the Hudson River and encompassing 42nd Street through the low 50s, Hell's Kitchen was a rough-hewn neighborhood where boys grew up speaking more with their fists than with words.

Sylvester's father, Frank Stallone, was born in Sicily and came to the U.S. with his family when he was a young boy. He was raised in an environment of Old World values, by parents who were proud and extremely ethical. As in most immigrant families,

Frank's father was the unquestioned head of the household.

Frank joined the army when he was a young man and upon his discharge returned to New York. With an aquiline face and piercing eyes, he toyed briefly with the notion of becoming an actor. However, after working in a few amateur shows, he gave it up because he was simply too nervous when he had to go onstage. Instead, he decided to apply his considerable charm and outgoing personality in another direction, by studying to become a hairdresser. Shortly after beginning an apprenticeship, he met and fell in love with Jacqueline Labofish, who was one of Billy Rose's Longstemmed Roses, the famed chorines who kicked up their heels at the Diamond Horseshoe Club.

The two youthful lovers could not have been less alike. Frank was friendly and articulate, but, because of his upbringing, he had a down-to-earth, very traditional nature. Jacqueline, on the other hand, was what Sylvester has unabashedly dubbed "an eccentric." Apart from being a chorus girl, a profession many considered to be somewhat slatternly, she was a devout believer in astrology and had a penchant for changing her hair color, sometimes from day to day.

Though they didn't know each other long and had very little money, Frank and Jacqueline married shortly after they met, moving into a cramped apartment on 9th Avenue at the northern fringe of Hell's Kitchen. It was a rundown place, but it was all they could afford.

The couple lived on Jacqueline's salary while Frank learned his trade. Things got very tight late in 1945 when Jacqueline discovered that she was pregnant and had to give up dancing. Her first child was born on July 6, 1946, by which time the family's finances were so low that she was forced to have the baby in the charity ward of a local hospital. Prophetically, the hospital was located on West 44th Street, across the street from the famous Actors Studio, whose alumni include Marilyn Monroe, Montgomery Clift, and Dustin Hoffman.

The baby was a boy, and Jacqueline had planned to call him Tyrone after Tyrone Power, her favorite film star. However, because the delivery had been an especially difficult one—the doctors had had to use forceps because of the size of the child—the woman was given tranquilizers and slept through the naming of her son. Frank had decided that instead of Tyrone he would give the boy two names from his side of the family: Sylvester Gardenzio. Though Jacqueline was angry when she learned what Frank had done, it was too late to undo it. Besides, when she took the child home there was more to worry about than just his name.

Noticing that the baby's left eye seemed to be drooping, they rushed him back to the hospital. A doctor examined him and, much to the physician's dismay, discovered that when the forceps had been used, too much pressure had been applied to one of the baby's major facial nerves, severing it. That meant the boy would be paralyzed over a considerable portion of that side of his face, including not only the area under the eye but that side of his lip, tongue, and chin as well.

The Stallones were upset, of course, but they had no recourse against the hospital. In any case, getting angry wouldn't help their son, and they resolved to deal with any problems as they occurred.

As it turned out, for the next two years neither Frank nor Jacqueline saw very much of Sylvester, or "Binky" as they called him. Since they both had to work, each Sunday night they would leave the boy with a woman in the neighboring borough of Queens, picking him up on Friday evenings and spending the weekend with him. It was a matter not of preference for the Stallones, but of necessity. Frank desperately wanted to save up enough money so that they could move from the city entirely, and this was the only way they could do it. Later, when asked just how poor his parents were when he was born, Sylvester would only half joke, "Poor? When you suckle a radiator for heat, that's *poor!*"

But worse than poverty, the lack of parental attention and supervision was to prove most detrimental to the youth.

Sylvester describes himself as having been "a kinetic child, always in motion and always in trouble." His earliest recollections of mischief making stretch back to when he was nearly four years old, when he remembers having decided one day that "all the cars on the block should be painted red, so I proceeded to do that." Indeed, cars became a frequent target of the young Stallone. He recalls that when he was not much older, if he happened to see a bug on the hood of a car, he'd "stamp him out with an iron pipe." Another time, early in his teenage years, he was walking down the street one night and noticed a car that reminded him of a tank. Letting his imagination get the better of him, Sylvester pretended that he was a soldier "being attacked by Rommel's tank corps," gathered up an armful of bricks, and proceeded to bomb the automobile until it was literally covered with dents. Though the owner came out "and nearly beat me to death," Sylvester felt no remorse for these activities, not because he was mean-spirited but because anything he did as part of a fantasy was more or less forgotten when he turned to something else.

Naturally, Frank didn't share his son's insouciance and had very little patience for the boy's behavior. When asked to describe his father in one word, Sylvester immediately says "stern," then adds with a wry smile, "I don't want to say I was mistreated, but the first thing my parents ever bought for me was a leash."

Sylvester overstates the case, but not by much. "Tough," he says, elaborating on his father and his Old World sensibilities. "Extremely tough. I've seen him eat a raw sparrow. It's true! Let's just say he communicated with, uh, *volatile* sign language. Our family was never like the Waltons where you sit down and explain. My father set the rule and I had to adhere to it. My father considered me a troublemaker, so I got brutal 'massages' (spankings)." He smiles mirthlessly. "The Mafia had the black hand; my father had the back hand."

Things got particularly bad for Sylvester when his younger brother was born in 1950. Though the boys have always been very close personally, Frank Jr. was always the beautiful, outgoing, good-humored baby and the apple of his parents' eye. Moreover, when he got older, Frank Jr. displayed a knack for music which his parents both lauded and encouraged. Not only did this give the younger boy self-esteem and attention, but music also provided him with an outlet for his energies. Sylvester could only get attention or blow off steam by acting wild, and, sadly, when the Stallones finally did introduce their eldest son to music, giving him saxophone lessons, it was not to provide him with a creative outlet but with the hope that playing the instrument would help to strengthen his facial muscles.

On his own, at the ripe old age of nine, Sylvester did manage to stumble onto creative satisfaction in painting, a pursuit he continues to enjoy as an adult. His works tended to be relatively literal when he was a child, becoming more abstract as he grew older; and while his father would look at the paintings and concede that his boy may have had raw talent, he simply never encouraged him the way he did his younger son. Sylvester has gone so far as to say that he felt "pounded down" by Frank Sr. and concludes, "I can't lie and say it was a wonderful childhood. It was terrible." It's a perception that Frank Jr. later echoed in a burst of bitter candor. "I hate my family, except my brother. Our parents were very inconsistent with us, and Sly went through much undue physical and emotional abuse from them." However, he is quick to add that "my brother and I were always close. We fought sometimes but we loved each other."

With the arrival of Frank Jr., it became imperative that the family finally leave Hell's Kitchen. There was no room for them all in the apartment, and Jacqueline didn't want Frank Jr. growing up in the streets, where Sylvester was spending more and more of his time. But at the same time they couldn't afford the prices elsewhere in the city or in the neighboring boroughs. After doing some checking, Frank Sr. decided to move his family to a three-story home in Silver Springs, Maryland, a pleasant suburb of Washington, D.C. There he opened his own beauty salon, called J. Frank Hair Stylists, and worked long hours to make it a success.

In moving to a more suburban atmosphere, he and his wife had hoped that Sylvester would change; predictably, he did not. He was five years old when they moved, and it was time to start school; if anything, that only made matters worse.

Because of his partially paralyzed mouth, Sylvester slurred his words, which made him extremely uncomfortable when he had to talk to other people. To this day, he says, "I've got what you'd call a Mafioso voice, and I'm very self-conscious about it." As a child he refused to talk to other children because of it. However, kids didn't hesitate to come over and talk to *him*—to taunt him because the left side of his face didn't move much. He says they called him "Slant Mouth" because he reminded them of "a Mister Potato Head with all the pieces in the wrong place" and were always asking if he ever used his mouth for an umbrella rack. They also harassed him because they thought he had a silly name. "The kids called me Sylvester Puddytat, Sylvester Tweetybird," he says, and when he refused to let that get to him, they simply

called him "wop." That made him mad because it
insulted not only him but his family, and it was the
cause of many brawls.

To top it all off, Sylvester was extremely thin and
had rickets. That put him at a disadvantage when it
came to athletics, and his insecurity at sports gave his
peers even more to tease him about. So he stayed
largely to himself and, in his words, "enjoyed my own
company and did a lot of fantasizing." He also took to
calling himself Sly, not only in the hopes of forestalling
the teasing but because he liked the connotations of
the word. He felt like a loner, like a fox, and the
nickname served to reinforce that identity in his mind.

Still, young Sylvester was not always as canny as he
could have been. In 1949, the comic book *Superboy*
was introduced, recounting the adventures of Superman as a child. Sylvester discovered it shortly thereafter, and the character became his hero and role model.
The two did indeed have a lot in common: both were
loners (Superboy couldn't afford to get close to anyone lest they discover his secret identity), and both
were picked on by their classmates (Superboy because
he pretended to be timid Clark Kent). In fact, so strong
was Sylvester's identification with the comic-book
character that when he was seven he even made a
costume using blue tights, red shorts, a sweatshirt
with a red S drawn on it, and a barber's smock from
his father's salon as a cape. He wore it under his
clothing and made the mistake of telling one of his
schoolmates what he'd done; the boy informed the
teacher, and the teacher, in an incredible display of
insensitivity, forced Sylvester to get up, undress, and

show the rest of the class his costume. The incident served no purpose but to convince the young boy that he should confide in no one and drove him further into his shell.

However, Sylvester did manage to come out long enough to join the Cub Scouts, since he liked the idea of doing good deeds and wearing the snappy blue uniform. In fact, it was during this time that Sylvester Stallone made his acting debut. He appeared in a show his den put on about Smokey the Bear, playing, as he puts it, "the lower half of the bear."

As it turned out, playing the bear would also be his *only* public performance during his childhood. Heartened by the fact that he'd finally been able to do something right, he tried out for the school play. Reading for the part of Mr. Toad in *Mr. Toad Goes West*, he had to affect a British accent and was all but hooted off the stage by his classmates. He would not try to act again for more than a decade.

Not surprisingly, with his head in the clouds and his social intercourse stunted, Sylvester posted an awful academic record. "I was not a good student," he says candidly, explaining, "I've never considered myself intelligent; I've considered myself clever." It was an important distinction, since what Sylvester regarded as canny or insightful his teachers often regarded as strange. Typical was his experience in sixth grade, when he would hand in his weekly compositions only to have his teacher hand them back week after week with a failing grade. That made him frustrated and angry. "I'd take a normal situation and fly with it," he explains. "Like, I'd do a 400-word essay on what it would be like to eat a car. And the teacher would write on my paper, 'But you can't eat a car.' And I'd say, 'But what if you could?' " Sylvester's teachers never understood his slightly diffracted way of looking at the world, and, as he puts it, "My grades went from bad to nonexistent, straight F. I could have laid in a coma and gotten better grades."

Meanwhile, outside the classroom, the older he got, the more his exploits took on a frenetic, dangerous edge. When he wasn't bombing cars with bricks or playing practical jokes on the kids who teased him— taping "kick me" signs to their backs or placing thumbtacks on their seats—he would do things like jumping from one roof to another or, in one instance, actually leaping off the roof with an open umbrella to see if the umbrella would cause him to float up like Mary Poppins. In that particular case he might well have suffered serious injury if his father hadn't been building a barbecue pit. The trough Frank Sr. had been using to mix cement was partially filled with water, and Sylvester happened to land in it. Sylvester says that when they heard the splash his parents came running out, and, seeing him in the water with the umbrella wrapped around his neck, his father said to his mother, "This boy will never become President. You've given birth to an idiot."

The problem, Sylvester realizes today, was not that he was inherently a bad child. On the contrary, he says, "I was an *inventive* child. But I didn't have a suitable artistic outlet. So everything came out in physical challenges. I had all the sensibilities of Quasimodo in those days. I must have broken about fourteen bones in my body doing things that were kind of adventurous." And the more he found gratification in physical activity, the more he turned to fighting. Any insult or smart remark would set him off, and he recalls, "I averaged a fight once every four or five weeks. Now when I reflect back on it, I know it was just a release of creative energy." Ironically, when these extremes of combat and isolationism became such a concern to his mother that she took him to a psychologist, Sylvester remembers the therapist remarking, "The kid's fine; do something about the parents."

As it happened, the therapist wasn't far off the mark. While Sylvester went his oddly merry way, his parents were having setbacks of their own. Professionally, things had gone extremely well for Frank Sr., who had parlayed his store into a chain of beauty salons which, according to Sylvester, made "a lot of money" and enabled the Stallones to move onto a farm. He'd also invested in real estate, and once he had the farm he raised horses which he either sold or used to play polo. The polo was especially important, Sylvester points out, because his father "wanted to be accepted into a certain class," and polo was an important part of that lifestyle.

For the young boy's part, when horses entered his life status was of no importance whatsoever; what mattered was that it was a sport he could do, and do extremely well. At the same time, it fanned the flames of his imagination as the erstwhile Superboy became the Lone Ranger. Without realizing it, Sylvester had found his calling. Thirty years later, riding remains one

of his favorite pastimes, and he is still playing super-
heroes.

Personally, however, things were not going at all
well for Frank Sr. and his wife. They argued frequently and tenaciously. As even the more tolerant
Frank Jr. puts it, he and his brother lived "in not a
happy household where it was every man for himself.
It was just unhappy." By 1957, the couple saw no
reason to continue the relationship, and, despite Frank
Sr.'s strong Catholic beliefs, they were divorced.
What's worse is that the arrangement they struck
regarding the boys was to prove extremely disruptive:
each parent would have custody of the children every
other year. Given his less intense nature and ability to
make new friends easily, Frank Jr. weathered the
annual uprooting relatively well. As for Sylvester,
things were about to go from bad to miserable.

# Chapter

## Two

When the Stallone marriage ended, Frank Sr. decided to remain in Maryland, while Jacqueline went to Philadelphia, settling in the lower-class northeast section of the city. There she took a new husband, a pizza maker. Though he was not the first prospective spouse the new Mrs. Filita had met since divorcing Frank Sr., all the others had been scared off by the increasingly wild nature of her eldest son.

Sylvester had gone from being a dreamer to someone who, in his words, was more like "a JD." He was not a delinquent in the purest sense of the word. Other youths didn't want him as part of their gangs, and nothing he did—from acting tough to being conciliatory to offering his peers gifts—could persuade them to accept the boy with the slurred voice and sad-looking eyes as their compatriot.

Meanwhile, Jacqueline made a decision that was to prove one of the most important in terms of her son. Never one to just sit around the house, she took a look around her new neighborhood and saw that there were countless gyms. Most were designed for men, many catered to boxers—world heavyweight champion Joe Frazier is from Philadelphia—and very few of these gyms were places where women could go. Always having been something of a fitness buff, the former chorus girl opened such an establishment herself.

At first, Sylvester had no interest in his mother's gym. The streets of Philadelphia held a junglelike fascination for the twelve-year-old, and rather than stay at home after school he would go exploring, poking around in junkyards, hanging out by the river, picking fights at the bowling alley if he was feeling restive, or just walking for block after block. Or else, whenever he had fifty cents in his pocket, he would go to the movies. Fittingly, it was in the dark of a movie theater that his interests were finally turned to weightlifting.

"The first time I saw *On the Waterfront,* I fell asleep," Sylvester recalls unabashedly. Marlon Brando meant nothing to him, and the tough but browbeaten characters Brando played left the young man cold. "But," Sylvester adds with boyish enthusiasm, "I practically tore the seats out of the theater when I saw my first Steve Reeves picture."

The year was 1959, and the picture that whipped Sylvester to a frenzy was *Hercules*. The teenager had always enjoyed action pictures like Kirk Douglas's *The Vikings* and Burt Lancaster's *The Crimson Pirate*. But *Hercules* star Steve Reeves was a former Mr. Universe, and the quick succession of sword-and-sandal epics he made—including *Hercules Unchained, Goliath and the Barbarians,* and *The Thief of Bagdad*—grabbed hold of Sylvester's imagination like nothing before. He wanted to *be* the screen superman. Happily, unlike his previous fascination with Superboy, the gym made it possible for Sylvester to do something about it.

When he got past the initial stage of fantasizing—swinging imaginary chains around his head like Hercules or beating up his brother with his fists or a makeshift sword—the thirteen-year-old had a serious talk with his mother about weightlifting. Jacqueline quickly agreed that it would be a good thing for her son to try, for not only did she subscribe to the credo that a fit body breeds a fit mind, but she was thrilled to see Sylvester finally enthused about something in a positive, constructive way.

Having him meet her at the gym after school one day, Jacqueline gave Sylvester an extra set of weights to cart home, and he began working out. Much to her delight, her son's interest proved to be more than a passing fancy. He kept at it every day, and what pleased her even more was that his fascination spread to other forms of athletics. When he knew he was looking good, he joined the track team at Lincoln High School, and, compensating for the shortness of his legs with unparalleled heart, he actually set records during his brief tenure at the school. Needless to say, the experience of desire overcoming a physical inadequacy was to have a profound impact on Sylvester's life and his work in film.

During the alternate years when Sylvester was with his father, he took the weights with him. It was one of the first times he could remember his father openly approving of something he was doing, though it was a backhanded compliment at best. When Sylvester broke out the weights, Frank Sr. remarked, "You weren't born with much of a brain, so you'd *better* develop your body." It was a line Sylvester never forgot, and it would be repeated word for word in *Rocky* to generate sympathy for the burly boxer.

Apart from giving him something to do, pumping iron and engaging in sports also worked wonders for Sylvester's crippled self-image. He had been to a total of twelve schools by the time he was fifteen years old, and he'd been thrown out of most because of his rebellious nature. In a Catholic school he attended while living with his father in Maryland, he was expelled for doing things like eating the tapioca desserts earmarked for the nuns and hiding crucifixes. Back in Philadelphia, three public schools all threw him out for setting fires in trashcans and decking kids who teased him about his name or his looks. Thanks to his newly beefed-up body, though, the taunting became less and less frequent.

Virtually everywhere Stallone went, he had the same problems with the faculty. He says bitterly, "I was told by my teachers that my brain was dormant, and I took it to heart." Luckily, he adds, he had weightlifting and "channeled a tremendous amount of energy" into his physical development, using it the way Frank Jr. used his guitar and his music as an outlet. By the time he was sixteen, he owned 16½-inch biceps and more confidence than he'd had during all the years he'd been snubbed and taunted by his peers.

Predictably, as Sylvester's interest in physical fitness blossomed, his academic performance went from bad to worse. Before, he hadn't any interest in it; now he had no time for it either. He freely admits, "I would go to school chiefly to flirt. The guys would be out throwing baseballs and I would be in there throwing one-liners." But before long, even the girls weren't enough to keep Sylvester interested in school, and the sixteen-year-old dropped out.

Sylvester's first thought was to join the navy, since it offered both a decent salary and the kind of virile adventure he thought he'd enjoy. But Frank Sr. convinced his son that he would not like the military discipline, and Sylvester briefly considered going to Australia to give sheepherding a try. However, in his very persuasive way, Frank Sr. urged Sylvester to try beauty school instead. To his credit, although the young man found the idea distasteful, he tried it for six months. During that time, he kept telling himself, "Oh boy, this isn't for me," since not only was the work physically unchallenging, but, he says, "My imagination was running wild with me." He needed to do something that wasn't quite so dull and finally threw in the towel during pincurl and finger-waving exercises. He returned to Philadelphia, deciding that even high school was preferable.

Convinced that a public school wasn't the best place

for Sylvester, Jacqueline went around looking at private schools until she found Manor High School. Run by the Devereaux Foundation in the Philadelphia suburb of Berwyn, Manor was a coed facility located on thirty-two sprawling acres and specialized in helping students who had learning problems or were not socially well adjusted. Enrollment was limited to one hundred pupils, with virtually every student meeting weekly with a psychotherapist.

Sylvester was impartial to the therapeutic benefits of the school, though he was gratified that they let him enroll as Mike Stallone so that he wouldn't have to put up with a new wave of Sylvester jokes. He was also impressed by the breadth of the high school's athletic program, and he actively partook in fencing, riding, boxing, and football. In fact, the gridiron team had a championship season during the year he played, star fullback Sylvester joking that Manor won primarily because "the other teams were afraid we'd freak out."

Yet, of everything that happened to him during his two years at the school, nothing was quite so memorable as the night he had sex for the first time—though not only because of the lovemaking itself. Continuing his flirting ways, Sylvester took as his partner the girlfriend of a fellow student. Going out on their historic date, the couple was unaware that the jealous boyfriend had followed. Spying on them, he assaulted the couple when it became apparent what Sylvester and the girl were doing. Not only did Sylvester get into trouble for fighting, but he was severely reprimanded by the school for doing so stark naked.

Though Sylvester's stay at Manor cost his parents more than $10,000, it was money well spent. Despite the occasional tussle, he did settle down somewhat as a result of the efforts of the staff and his own maturing, and in 1965 he was actually ready to give college a try.

Unfortunately, because of his abysmal academic record, no college was willing to give Sylvester a try. Thus, as she had when looking for a private school for Sylvester, Jacqueline launched a thorough search for a university that would accept her son. To her credit, she refused to be discouraged by countless rejections and, in particular, a profile of Sylvester that had been done after he was tested by the Drexel Institute of Technology in Philadelphia. Sylvester recalls, "My mother was told, 'Your son is suited to work in the area of elevator operations.' In other words, I'd be the guy who crawls through the trapdoor of an elevator to tighten the cables."

Learning that the American College in Leysin, Switzerland, was in need of money, she contacted the school and struck a deal which was extraordinary, to say the least. In exchange for their admitting Sylvester, she agreed to pay his full year's tuition in advance, money the school could keep if her son failed to make the grade. Naturally, this put a lot of pressure on the young man, but, as he was beginning to discover, he functioned at his best when the heat was on. His mother also instructed Sylvester to send her weekly reports on what he was doing, not only because she was interested in his progress but because, as she candidly admits, she wished she could be in Leysin herself, enjoying the scenery and clean air 4500 feet up in the foothills of the Alps. Instead, she lived vicariously through her son.

Though Sylvester didn't set any houses on fire scho-

lastically, neither did he do as badly as school officials
had feared. He did just enough to make the grade in
math, science, and history, though he did surprisingly
well in art and literature. He was just beginning to
discover the joys of reading, dipping into everything
from Hemingway to Dos Passos.

For the most part, however, his interests at the age
of nineteen were money and women, and he was
always on the lookout for ways to make both. The
women came easy—Sylvester's nickname at the
school was Studly, quite a contrast to his Sylvester
Puddytat days—and, in time, so did the money. Be-
friending fellow student Prince Paul of Ethiopia, whom
he rescued from a bunch of students who were picking
on him, the industrious Sylvester used the monarch's
money to open a fast-food operation in the garage
of a chalet. There he began peddling a concoction he
called "vacheburgers," a patty that was "part lamb,
part beef, and part sawdust." His rationale was that
Americans would be homesick for American food, and
he was right. Business flourished, and he eventually
had to give it up because it was simply too time-
consuming.

Instead, he found a way to combine his two favorite
pursuits, taking a job as proctor at the girls' dormitory.
With a wicked smile he refers to that position as "fox-
in-the-henhouse time," not only because he availed
himself of the ladies but because he also charged
fellow students two francs each if they wanted a peek
at the girls, and demanding five francs an hour for
every boy who wanted to spend some time alone with
a girlfriend. He also had a lucrative sideline teaching

his peers how to feign an asthma attack so they could get out of classes. The price of these valuable lessons was $20 per student.

Remarkably, Sylvester's inventive sidelines went undetected by the faculty and directors of the school, to the extent that on one occasion the school actually assigned him to chaperone a group of girls on a trip to Paris. Once there, Sylvester found a cheap hostel for them and pocketed the difference. "What the hell," he says with a shrug. "They saw the real Paris that way."

The one genuinely aboveboard means he had of making money during his two years at the school was by teaching boxing. Ever since he'd seen *The Champion* with Kirk Douglas, Sylvester had been fascinated with pugilists. Walking around the streets of Philadelphia, he'd stick his head into the gyms, watch the fighters work out, occasionally put on gloves himself. He'd boxed in several of the schools he'd attended, and in Switzerland he fought again. He confesses that he wasn't terribly good, saying that the best fight he'd ever had "was one with the heavyweight champion of the Rhodesian police where I got lucky. I knocked him down in the first round, couldn't believe it, but he got up and knocked out my cheap mouthpiece and chopped me up around the mouth. He cut me up, so they stopped it after two rounds."

But Sylvester was an excellent coach and was able to inspire other students with the same kind of "go-for-it" psychology he'd seen at his mother's gym.

Given his various activities, Sylvester didn't have much leisure time. He acknowledges that he dabbled in the sixties "meditation thing," having been primed for the bizarre by his mother's preoccupation with astrology, but for the most part he spent his waking hours trying to earn money and score creditable grades. Yet, the one pursuit for which he did make time was acting.

There was an excellent drama club at the American College, and, with the humiliation of Mr. Toad long forgotten, Sylvester tried out for their presentation of Arthur Miller's *Death of a Salesman*. He recalls that the drama teacher said of his reading that it was "not bad for a guy who looks like a Neanderthal," and he landed the part of Biff, son of the ill-fated traveling salesman, Willy Loman. What he discovered when he first read his lines aloud was that he "liked the gratification of making words come alive. It came naturally for me." And in a perverse way he felt vindicated; he'd been vilified for pretending to be Superboy and had been regarded as an oddball because he wanted to be Hercules. Here, at last, his fantasies were legitimized. He could be whomever he wanted and not have to feel ashamed for it. He also discovered the catharsis of acting. Biff enabled him to express emotions he had never revealed to himself or anyone else. As Sylvester puts it, "I knew I could immerse myself in the part, especially when I give my mother the flowers and she won't accept them because I've left my father in a barroom toilet." He had always been able to express joy on the rare occasions when he felt it, but now he could also express long-suppressed emotions from hatred to disappointment without feeling guilt. And, as he discovered after his triumphant portrayal of Biff, he could get a standing ovation for doing it.

Not that *Death of a Salesman* was an unqualified success for the budding actor. He recalls that during one performance he "picked up those flowers in one hand and a radio in the other, and I threw the radio against the canvas wall. It collapsed and there were the stagehands, drinking beer, puffing on 'hot dogs,' and sniffing glue. It was a comedy sensation."

Despite the fact that he was constantly doing something, Sylvester felt very much alone in Switerland. During vacations he took forays into Spain and France, but these were primarily solitary ventures which failed to stir him once he got past the novelty of seeing new places. The loneliness that had been forced on him as a child wasn't even as bad as this. He'd had his anger to fulfill him then; here, there was nothing.

Recognizing that he needed a fresh challenge, and also realizing that he'd gotten that challenge on the stage, Sylvester applied to the University of Miami. He was accepted as a drama major and in 1969 left Switzerland to complete his education.

In much the same way Sylvester had devoted himself to weight lifting, he threw himself into acting. However, performing was not like athletics, where the participant either won or lost; acting was governed by opinion, and almost from the start the school's opinion of Sylvester was negative. He complains, "They were saying to me, 'Quit! You stink! You're bad!' " Nor was it just that they thought his acting was bad. They looked down their noses at his broad-shouldered physical type ("They told me I was out of step because beach pictures had run their course") and had an even lower opinion of his blossoming writing abilities.

Sylvester had taken to writing playlets, and the school wouldn't let him perform them or even audition reading his own material. Sylvester was stunned; it had been his understanding that the drama department was supposed to encourage creativity, not stifle it. As a result, he says, "I succumbed to depression," a slate-gray shroud that hung over him for his first few months at the university. His disappointment was exacerbated by the fact that he had also tried out for the football team and had been rejected. The school that he'd hoped would be a panacea was turning out to be exactly the opposite.

However, Sylvester was beginning to learn that brooding didn't get him anywhere, and, deciding "to fight back," he read through thick stacks of plays and found material that appealed to him, works like Israel Horovitz's outré *Rats*. Then, organizing a "splinter" acting group, he put on shows in the basement of a local church or, when that was unavailable, in students' garages. His stagings won a small but devoted following, among the most gratifying achievements of his life, and persuaded Sylvester that he wasn't as worthless as his instructors seemed to think. In fact, working on his own, Sylvester became so convinced that he was a good actor that in the fall of 1969, three credits shy of earning a college diploma, he quit school. Packing his bags, he headed for New York, determined to become a professional actor and show the world that no one could stifle Sylvester Stallone.

# Chapter
## Three

Sylvester had never shied away from hard work and long hours, and that was good. Once he hit New York, he found himself burning the candle not only at both ends but in the middle as well.

Stopping off to see his mother before continuing on to the Great White Way, he sat for her while she did his horoscope. According to her prognostication, he would struggle as an actor for seven years, fail, and finally succeed as a writer. Sylvester put a great deal of credence in astrology, and, taking her prediction seriously, he decided to hedge his bets. He'd never written a screenplay, of course, but Sylvester was undaunted. Thinking back to *Easy Rider*, which was the last movie he'd seen, he says, "I figured I couldn't write any worse," and as soon as he'd settled into a room at New York's Sutton Hotel, he went out and bought a book about screenplays in order to learn the correct form. By day he would go for interviews, and by night he would write, often falling asleep at his desk.

The Sutton was hardly an inspiring environment for writing or for anything else. Sylvester told *The New York Times* that he used to call it the Slutton, and he had a room so small "you could lie in your bed and stretch out your arms and open the door, shut the window, turn on a faucet. You never had to move." But in short order he did manage to produce his first script, an opus with the rather unwieldy title *Cry Full, Whisper Empty, In the Same Breath*. He will say little about his Dylanesque script, remarking only that it was never even read by any of the producers he sent it to—"not with *that* title." Which, he adds, was "just as well, because it was really awful."

His next effort fared no better. Called "Sad Blues," it was the saga of a pop singer (presumably modeled loosely after Frank Jr.) who has a heart condition which can only be cured by eating bananas. During the course of the screenplay, the musician falls in love and is ultimately rejected. Disconsolate, he goes onstage one night without having had his day's ration of bananas and promptly keels over. At that point, having had a change of heart, his ex-girlfriend comes running into the theater with an armful of the life-sustaining fruit. Though she's too late to save her lover's life, he dies contentedly in her arms.

This script too was not exactly what producers were

looking for, and it failed to sell. Undaunted, Sylvester continued to scratch out new works on yellow pads whenever he had the time and quickly produced his third script, "Till Young Men Exit," for which there were also no takers. However, this one was considerably more ingenious than the other two, the story of a group of frustrated actors who kidnap a Broadway producer and hold him for ransom, only to have him die while he's in their custody. No wonder: to underscore their contempt for the pop crap he produces, the actors had placed their captive on a strict diet of Fizzies and Kool-Aid.

Though these early scripts were all about the kind of nihilistic failures who populated the films of the day, Sylvester wasn't terribly surprised when none of them sold. Although Sylvester often felt like a nihilistic failure, inside he was still Hercules fighting alongside Jason and his Argonauts. Losers just didn't hold much appeal for him, and it showed in his writing.

Unfortunately, Sylvester didn't fare much better with acting. Since he wanted to make it on the New York stage, he wouldn't consider offers to work in summer stock or in road companies. As a result, he couldn't get a union card, which meant that the only auditions he was permitted to attend were the so-called open auditions, where anyone with an urge to act was given a try—along with an appropriately curt dismissal if they weren't what the director wanted. Over the years, Sylvester would manage to build up a thick skin where rejection was concerned, especially when he heard himself repeatedly pigeonholed as a "Brando type." He didn't see himself in that downtrodden light and is quick to add that, in any case, even when he did go to auditions calling for characters of the "torn-shirt, dirty-Levis school," he wasn't hired.

Despite his pragmatism, Sylvester admits than on occasion frustration would get the better of him. A standout was the day he tried out for an off-Broadway production of *Fortune and Men's Eyes,* a play about homosexuality in prison. The director was former actor Sal Mineo, who, after watching Sylvester storm across the stage, tossing chairs aside and shoving crew members around, casually informed him that he wasn't right for the part of a bitter, seething convict. Sylvester looked over, certain that Mineo was wrong. Sylvester has always been very blunt about what he can and can't do. As he puts it, with an edge of sarcasm, "I don't polish my craft. I don't tune my instrument. I'm not an oboe or a bass fiddle, and I don't sit up all night sipping brandy and brooding about motivation. Either I can do it or I can't." And in this case, he knew he could play the part.

Bubbling with rage, Sylvester stood his ground for a moment, then jumped toward Mineo, stopping inches from his face, wagging a menacing finger under his nose and glowering.

"Now say it!" he demanded. "Tell me I'm not intimidating!" Shaken, the director admitted that the actor was intimidating, and Sylvester backed away. He still didn't get the part, but he certainly felt better for having given Mineo something to chew on.

Coincidentally, the part he'd failed to get was playing a character named Rocky.

Sylvester only managed to land one part during the

first few months he was in New York, winning a
featured role as the monstrous Minotaur in *Desire
Caught by the Tail,* the only play ever written by
Picasso. *Desire Caught by the Tail* ran for three weeks
in the Bronx, playing to an average of seven people a
night, and of all the performances they gave Sylvester
says that only one was memorable. To try and spice up
the play, one of the actors decided to spray the mon-
ster with a fire extinguisher. Sylvester took the $CO_2$
flush in the face and had to be rushed to a hospital,
where, he says icily, "they thawed my face out with a
heat lamp."

Too proud to borrow money from home, Sylvester
was broke by May of 1970, and, moving from the
Sutton, he took up residence among the homeless who
meander in and out of the Port Authority Bus Terminal
on Manhattan's seamy West 42nd Street. "I was literally starving," he recalls, having used his last quarter
to store his books, pencils, and notebooks in a locker.
However, he still checked the trade papers each day,
and it was through a notice in one of them that he
learned of a part in a pornographic film entitled *Party
at Kitty and Studs.* He looked into it and says, "They
wanted to know if I'd take off my clothes. 'Why not?' I
said. 'I take them off for free at home every night.'"

Despite his glib attitude, it obviously wasn't the kind
of work Sylvester wanted to take. But the producers
were offering him $100 a day, and he was "cold and
sick and broke and on the very brink of committing a
criminal act." So he did the film, which has even less
of a plot than most pornographic films—and less titilla-
tion as well. Though full-frontal nudity abounds and

there is a lot of thrashing and panting, none of the men is ever visibly aroused.

Sylvester starred as the narcissistic Studs, who, though he loves his partner Kitty (Henrietta Holm), has a highly active libido which he sates by getting together four other promiscuous people after announcing a party on a bulletin board. The rest of the film consists of the resultant orgy, Sylvester's revels including a shower scene with Kitty (she's delighted when the soap falls so she can bend down and "get closer to my favorite part of your body") and the entire cast partaking in an erotic version of *Ring a Ring o' Roses*. As it turned out, the picture was so awful, even by the undemanding standards of the skin industry, that it was never released.

Only after Sylvester became a star in *Rocky* did *Party at Kitty and Studs* finally surface. Reportedly, the actor was offered the negative of the film for $100,000, but he refused to pay, telling the producers to "hit the pike" and condemning extortion at any price. Initially, says Sylvester, the producers "marketed that piece of scum in Hollywood, [getting] $10,000 rental to show it at private parties." He put the best possible face on an unpleasant situation. "Hell, for $100,000 forget the film. I'll be there myself!" The picture subsequently played the pornographic houses in New York and was eventually released on videocassette as *The Italian Stallion*, under which name it is presently available.

With $200 in his pocket, Sylvester got himself a new place. Located over an abandoned delicatessen on 56th Street and Lexington Avenue, it cost only $71 a month and, while worse than the Sutton, was better than the bus terminal. The only working sink was in the bathroom—the bathtub and toilet belonged to the cockroaches—and, since there was no oven, any cooking he did was on a hotplate. Whenever he ate what he cooked he did so on the floor, as the only furniture he owned was the crate on which he did his writing. He didn't even have a bed, sleeping on an old coat he'd spread on the floor. When he wanted to wash the coat, or any of his other clothes, he did so by taking a shower with his clothes on.

Still, it was a roof over his head, and to make sure it stayed there, he decided to put his priorities in order. The first thing he did was cut his costs. He didn't bother installing a phone and had the electricity cut off, writing by candlelight. Moreover, having learned that starvation wasn't for him, he went the route of many actors, taking part-time jobs which would pay the rent and leave him free to go to auditions. Naturally, his heart wasn't in any of these jobs, and he never lasted long. One week he worked as a salad maker, another he was cutting open fish at a midtown delicatessen, the next he worked as a delivery boy, then it was on to cooking pizzas. His most unusual job during this period was cleaning the lion cages at Central Park Zoo for $1.12 an hour, employment he himself terminated when a lion urinated on his leg, ruining Sylvester's only pair of pants. "Let me tell you," he says, "they're accurate up to fifteen feet!"

His longest job during this period was one he kept even while he worked elsewhere, serving as bouncer at the apartment house. He says, "It was my job to oust the bums and beggars who slept in the lobby and halls." He hated to do that, he says. "For good luck, I used to drop a coin in one of their tin plates before going in for an audition. It became a habit," he says, even though he knew "it wasn't right, because every time you give beggars money, you're only reinforcing their problem. You're making it so they don't have to go to work." Not that these philosophical ramifications occurred to him at the time. He came to this conclusion years later, when he went back to the building and saw that a number of the bums he used to know were still there. Even so, before leaving, he gave each of them a coin for good luck.

One of the last jobs Sylvester held during this period was also his most inspired and lucrative, working as an usher at Walter Reade's Baronet Theater.

To be sure, there were disadvantages to ushering. The crowds could be large and abusive, and he hated the uniform he had to wear. The blue pants were always too short, and every time he donned a jacket it still smelled around the armpits from the usher who'd worn it before. To make matters worse, the pay was only $37 a week. But Sylvester quickly found a way to pad his income by scalping tickets to hot films. Approaching latecomers who had obviously made a long trek from out of town, he would offer them tickets and let them in ahead of the crowd for $20 or $30, depending upon how affluent they looked. For the two weekends he was working, the superhit *M\*A\*S\*H* was playing and Sylvester pocketed $600 a weekend; unfortunately, the scam came to an end when he approached a wealthy-looking gentleman in a white suit and said, "Hey, for twenty bucks I can get you a good seat."

Playing with the red carnation on his lapel, the man looked up and replied, "Hey, for nothing I can get you your walking papers. I'm Walter Reade."

Though Sylvester's days as an usher came to a swift, unpleasant end, his two-week tenure had been exceptional in that he had met a beautiful blond ticket girl from Chester, Pennsylvania, who was also an aspiring actor. Her name was Sasha Czach, and she was the first girl he'd dated since coming to New York. "Who could afford a social life?" he asks. "You couldn't say to some girl, 'Hey, let's go to the park.' She'd say, 'But it's snowing.'" Besides, he adds, all his free time was taken up looking for work.

While Sylvester still couldn't afford to go out, Sasha literally took his breath away. "She was taking tickets at the Baronet," he says, "and wearing a lowcut black thing—they dressed the usherettes that way to entice people in—and I walked over and said, 'I think I love you.'" Not knowing Sylvester and his impulsive ways, Sasha regarded the pronouncement as a line. Nor did he look like the kind of guy she particularly wanted to date. At the time, he was on his way to work and wearing the coat that doubled as his bed, which he describes as "a greasy sheepskin coat that was so old it leaked; I had to put Vaseline on it to keep it waterproofed." He also had shoulder-length hair which he promptly went home and cut, intent on wooing this girl. Sasha acknowledges that he didn't do a bad job of cleaning up, considering that he'd given himself the haircut by candlelight, using cuticle scissors.

Over the next few days, Sasha found out just how sincere Sylvester was. He was witty, deferential, a little goofy, and totally endearing. They went out and continued to see each other even after Sylvester was abruptly asked to turn in his jacket.

The remainder of the first half of 1970 was one of professional torpor and personal poverty for Sylvester. He continued to work odd jobs, but these were increasingly difficult to hold as he tried to get to every audition he could. He also tested endlessly for TV commercials, never landing a single one. He vividly remembers going for a toothpaste commercial, despite the fact that he's always felt his smile looks "cruel," only to have his worst fears confirmed when the director asked, "What did you do, just kill a baby?" Agent Rhonda Young recalls another dead-end interview: "I sent him to Ivory Soap. They were looking for a greaser, but they sent him back. They said there was a limit to seediness."

The high point of this period was landing work as an extra in *Lovers and Other Strangers,* the film that marked the screen debut of Diane Keaton. Sylvester didn't have a single line in the film and is barely visible onscreen. But it was the first time he got to see a professional film crew in action, and he found it exciting. It was exactly the kind of jolt he needed just then, for he was beginning to despair of ever making his mark as an actor or a writer.

Looking back on that period, Sylvester considers it valuable that he'd had to struggle, not only because it toughened his professional skin but because it gave him a unique perspective about people. He spent a

great deal of time traveling to and from auditions by
subway, and there he discovered what he calls his
philosophy about people. Looking at their faces, he
realized, "They had no hope. They had no *heroes*."
Considering that, and also thinking about how badly
his downbeat screenplays had done, he began to form
an idea in the back of his mind of someday giving
people a hero or two who would mean as much to them
as Steve Reeves and Kirk Douglas had meant to him.

During the summer of that year, faced once again
with starvation, Sylvester tried out for an off-Broadway play entitled *Score*. Once again he was asked to
strip for his craft; only this time the producers were
offering union scale, a very serious enticement. The
play was about a swinging married couple trying to
persuade another married couple to swap mates with
them. The only other character in the play was a
telephone repairman who becomes sexually entangled
with the lot of them. That was the part for which
Sylvester auditioned, and he got it after reading a few
lines from the script and walking bare-chested across
the stage, demonstrating how impressive his chest
looked when fully expanded. As the show's writer–
director, Jerry Douglas, told author Marsha Daly,
Sylvester "gave a good audition and also happened to
have a good body." He adds that the actor "was a
dream" to work with, "creative and very professional." Costarring with Sylvester—who billed himself
as Sylvester E. Stallone to make the name more
unusual and, hence, unforgettable—were Michael
Beirne, Claire Wilbur, Lynn Swan, and Ben Wilson,
all of whom also cavorted naked onstage.

After a lengthy preview period—during which time
critics don't review a play, leaving the public to pay its
money and take its chances—*Score* opened at the
Martinique Theater on October 28. It was roasted by
the press and only managed to eke out twenty-three
performances before closing. However, Sylvester
came away from the debacle more or less content.
He'd received an excellent review from the show-
business journal *Variety*, which crowed, "The best
performance is given by Sylvester E. Stallone as the
comically lecherous, lower-middle-class repairman."
It wasn't much, but after the year he'd just been
through, the notice was the equivalent of an Oscar.

Sylvester continued to see Sasha, and one of his
great joys in life was to be with her each night. In 1971,
she would finally move in with him and give up her
own dreams to become an actress in order to work
full-time as a waitress; it was important to her that
Sylvester be able to go to auditions or work on his
screenplays. Her job also enabled the couple to eat
better than they were accustomed to, Sasha's boss
allowing her to take home food that was a day or two
shy of spoiling.

During this period, Sylvester also spent many days
reading. He had never been enamored of books, but he
knew that to write well one had to read. He notes that
the library was often warmer than his apartment,
which added to its appeal. Surprisingly, during this
period he found himself drawn to Puritan literature as
well as the works of Edgar Allan Poe, and he become
hooked on the poet's dark and tortured but strangely
beautiful imagery. Sylvester even lavished a great deal

of time writing a screenplay based on the life of Poe, one he insists he will one day bring to the screen with himself as the poet. Traditionalists have trembled on hearing exactly how he would play Poe. ("It would be a radical departure from the traditional view that he was a groveling dipsomaniac with iambic pentameter dripping from his lips," says Sylvester. "I would play him with a great roguish abandon, in the vein of *Tom Jones*.") However, the actor insists he would never do anything to dishonor the poet's memory, adding with a dash of pathos, "I can identify with Poe's tragic loss of people, his drive and his loneliness."

Like 1970, 1971 was a year of disappointment for Sylvester. He managed to get in with a distinguished, way-off-Broadway group called the Extension, but the catch was that no one got paid. They acted because agents and producers came and their work was seen. Sylvester wasn't one of the lucky ones, and nothing came of his efforts. He also got to put in a day's work on Jane Fonda's film *Klute*, albeit, once again, only as an extra. His contribution to Woody Allen's *Bananas* was slightly more rewarding since, although he still didn't have any dialogue, he did get to mug an old lady in a subway car in plain view of the camera. As far as his résumé went, he finally had a legitimate screen credit.

In the meantime, Frank Jr. had parlayed his musical talents into a blossoming career, and Sylvester and Sasha frequently went to the local clubs where he played with his group, Valentine. Though Frank had leapfrogged ahead of Sylvester, succeeding to a greater degree in an equally difficult profession, there was no envy on the part of his older brother. Sylvester was proud of the twenty-one-year-old, while Frank regarded his older brother as a very strong, very compassionate "father figure." It's a relationship that continues to be supportive and tight to this day.

Though Sylvester was far from prolific on screen and stage, he continued to keep himself extremely busy as a writer. He would compose all of his scripts in longhand, and at night Sasha would type them; or else he would dictate them to her and they would talk about the work as he went along.

At first it was a difficult collaboration. Sasha reveals, "He can be very explosive, especially when he's working on a script, and his temperament required constant attention." She finally came to understand that "the anger wasn't directed at me," but bringing him down from a fit inspired by disappointment or creative gridlock often required the patience of Mother Theresa. Sylvester may not dwell on character motivation when he's playing a part, but when he's writing it's a different story. "The writer is the entire nervous system, spine, and shoulders of a play or film," he says. Thus, he isn't satisfied until he sweats blood on each and every page.

As before, none of the scripts he wrote was bought for the screen. However, the more he wrote and the more he moved through New York, the more he was drawn to fiddle with characters cut from a heroic mold—as he describes it, "a representative of the common man." Nothing he wrote struck him as being perfectly representative of those ideals, but he knew that when he found such a character he might well have the key to the success that was eluding him.

In the meantime, he continued to read and audition while Sasha continued to waitress, and 1972 came and went like the years before it, without money or hope or a decent role in the offing.

# Chapter
## Four

As Sylvester entered his fourth year as a professional—and hungry—actor-writer, he went through
periods of severe doubt sandwiched between stretches
of creative passion.

Typical of the latter was the day when he literally
wrote a half-dozen thirty-minute TV scripts in a single
day. To ensure absolute privacy, he painted his apartment windows black and didn't leave the room until he
was done. Of that full day's output, he managed to sell
one of the scripts, a Poe-like horror opus, to the
anthology TV series "Touch of Evil." He was paid a
modest $2500 for his efforts. Thereafter, locking out
the world became more or less the way Sylvester
would write. After allowing an idea to gestate in the

back of his mind, he would literally pour it onto the paper in a fit of creative passion. Then he'd go back and fine tune it in subsequent drafts.

"In the first draft I always try for a skeletal structure," Sylvester explains. "Then I begin to inject humor and idiosyncrasies. You know, I just don't believe these guys who say it takes them nineteen years to write something. I just force myself to put it down and get it done." He adds, as only a blue-collar hero like Sylvester Stallone can, "I'm astounded by people who take eighteen years to write something. That's how long it took that guy to write *Madame Bovary*. And was that ever on a bestseller list? No. It was a lousy book and it made a lousy movie."

Though as a literary critic Sylvester made a terrific butcher, he managed to sell a few more scripts to TV during the year. But a big-screen sale still eluded him, and, driven by that frustration, he wrote what is perhaps one of his most scathing and certainly most unusual screenplays, *The Bogus Kingdom*. In this variation of the theme he'd explored in *Till Young Men Exit*, a group of down-and-out performers kidnap several powerful producers, use the talent of confederates in the makeup world to disguise themselves as those producers, and then take over the entertainment media, making it a better place for all.

*The Bogus Kingdom* never really had a chance, of course. The industry doesn't like to castigate itself, and as a rule pictures of that type have traditionally done poorly at the box office. However, the script allowed Sylvester to crystallize many of the diverse and unformed thoughts he had about why the film industry was experiencing a period of drought at the box office. As he later explained it, "I think the primary objective of creative art—of *film* art—is to create simplistic stories that touch everyone and affect their lives through giving them heroes, through answering questions." He went on, almost contemptuously, to say that while his own scripts had traces of autobiography, they were like parables, whereas "most directors today have opted for using the screen as a sounding board for their own psychological demons. They're putting their ulcers up on the screen, and that," he concluded, "is *wrong*. People don't want to go to the movies to think, and they don't want to go to see realism. They can see realism every day on the street for nothing." However, no one was turning over the reins of a major studio to Sylvester E. Stallone, and so his scripts and his vision remained unproduced and unrealized.

In the entertainment world, it's axiomatic that success has a way of creeping up on people when they don't actively pursue it. Sylvester got his first meaty film role that way—though, as if the fates were reluctant to snap his string of bad luck, it was a role he was forced to complete over a period of two years.

It was the fall of 1972, and Sylvester was actually on the verge of giving up acting. He and a friend had pooled their money to make a short, 16 mm film to use as a presentation piece. Entitled *Horses,* it was the story of a cowboy and an Indian who return from the dead in 1973 and are so disgusted by what they see that they go back to the grave. Not one producer ever saw *Horses;* in fact, says Sylvester, it was "so bad that my parents actually walked out of the room—and they'll normally sit through two hours of flower slides." Discouraged, he was busy making plans to go into another line of work when he got a call from his *Horses* costar. The friend wanted to know if Sylvester would go with him to drama class and read the other part in a scene he was going to do from *Death of a Salesman*. Sylvester agreed, and he did so well that the drama coach offered him a scholarship at the school. But Sylvester graciously refused, stating that he'd decided to give up acting and pursue work as an elevator repairman. Running back to the apartment, upset because the performance had reminded him how much he loved acting, he was surprised to receive a telegram (he still didn't have a phone) from a young producer named Stephen Verona who had seen his reading and was offering him something more tangible than a scholarship: a part in a film he was preparing to make. The money wasn't great—$2000—but the offer was just what Sylvester's ego needed. Having dashed to a pay phone to call Verona, Sylvester agreed to do his first screen role, playing the dull-witted Stanley Rosiello in *The Lords of Flatbush.*

*The Lords of Flatbush* was a look at the lives and loves of four teenage gang members in the late fifties. Boasting a sensitive and funny script, it also had a fine cast that included then-unknowns Henry Winkler, Susan Blakely, and Perry King, actors who brought a great deal of vitality and humanity to the project.

Unfortunately, what the film didn't have was much of a budget. Shooting in 16 mm as if it were a film-school project, producer–writers Verona and Martin

Davidson raised the entire $400,000 themselves, but they didn't have the money on hand at one time. Thus, while the film went before the cameras in Brooklyn in November of 1972, it shut down five weeks thereafter when the initial $50,000 ran out, and the cast and crew had to reassemble whenever there was enough money for the filmmakers to continue. Davidson says that in the interim he would show the completed footage to friends and family and ask for the funds to shoot some more, and even went door to door in the Flatbush area of Brooklyn, where he reports that, more often than not, residents were so taken with the project that they would actually "write checks out on their kitchen tables, on the oilcloth."

The film stopped and started three times during 1972–1974, a schedule that weighed heaviest on Sylvester. Not only did the salary fail to put an end to his poverty, but he had beefed himself up considerably to play the huge Stanley—his 5-foot 10-inch figure tipping the scales at a whopping 225 pounds—and had to maintain that overly muscled look for the duration. He admits, "I was never without a pint of ice cream in my hand and another one hidden away in a thermal bag tucked inside my motorcycle jacket. I was constantly eating, eating, eating to get this look." That also meant spending a lot of time at the gym to which he'd belonged off and on since coming to New York, in order to keep the ice cream from turning into pure fat. Though at times he would have preferred to be home writing instead of working out, he knew that Stanley might well be his only shot at the big screen, and if that were the case he wanted people to look back at the film

one day and think well of the unknown by the name of
Sylvester Stallone.

Throughout the intermittent shooting of *The Lords
of Flatbush*, Sylvester continued to go to countless
auditions, and one of these landed him another major
role in a minor film. The movie was *No Place to Hide*.
Filmed in New York on an extremely low budget, it
was the story of student Jerry Savage (Sylvester) who
must choose between a lovely country girl, Laurie
(Rebecca Grimes), and his career as an urban terrorist
whose latest project is blowing up a New York sky-
scraper. A gritty but superficial picture, *No Place to
Hide* managed to go unreleased for two years, after
which it surfaced and died a swift death. Discouraged
by the fate of the picture, Sylvester found himself
thankful for the start-and-stop schedule of *The Lords
of Flatbush*, since it gave him a chance not only to act
but to return to a character he'd grown to love. In fact,
he took it so much to heart that he even asked the
producers for permission to write extra lines for several key scenes, lines that suggested ambition and
hope beneath the loutish exterior. His contributions
were most notable in the engagement scene, in which
his tough, independent lug of a character is cajoled by
his pregnant girlfriend Frannie (Maria Smith) into buy-
ing her an expensive engagement ring. Sylvester is
brilliant in the scene, and the pièce de résistance—
Stanley's admonition to the jeweler that he'd drop him
if he ever again showed his girlfriend a $1600 piece of
jewelry—is delivered with that balance of vulnerability and power that has become a Stallone trademark.
In its review of the picture, *Time* magazine would call

this "the movie's best scene [in which] Stallone's face goes through a generation of changes," and his input to the screenplay was deemed so vital that Sylvester was freely given screen credit for "additional dialogue," a tribute rarely accorded anyone without long and acrimonious arbitration.

For the record, *The Lords of Flatbush* also contains the first of Sylvester's many screen slugfests, with Stanley manfully going hit for hit with Chico (Perry King). The match ends in a draw, the first and only time that a Stallone fight would do so.

When *The Lords of Flatbush* was finally completed, Verona and Davidson took it to various studios. Columbia finally agreed to release it, paying the young filmmakers $150,000 up front for the privilege. Less than a year before, George Lucas's *American Graffiti* had opened and become one of the top-grossing movies of all time; Columbia felt this picture had a lot of those same teenage rites-of-passage qualities. Blown up to professional-caliber 35 mm film, the picture opened to generally favorable reviews and brought an impressive $4,265,000 into the studio's coffers, money which Columbia split 50–50 with the determined young producers. Ironically, some of the film's strongest grosses were registered at the Baronet in Manhattan.

Sylvester earned the finest reviews of anyone in the cast. Typical was the notice in *Time* magazine, which went on to call Sylvester's performance "truly exceptional." Yet it was Henry Winkler who was tabbed to star in the new TV series *Happy Days,* and Susan Blakely and Perry King who won leading roles in the

major TV miniseries *Rich Man, Poor Man,* while
Sylvester continued to struggle. He was more resigned
than bitter, especially after being kept on tenterhooks
while there was talk about him starring in *Flatbush
Abroad,* in which newlyweds Stanley and Frannie win
a European vacation on *Let's Make a Deal.* But the
plans for a sequel fell through, as did talk of a possible
TV series based on the film, and the only work Sylvester could get was playing yet another mugger. This
time it was the film version of Neil Simon's hit comedy
*The Prisoner of Second Avenue,* and even that ended
unhappily. In his brief scene, Sylvester lifts Jack Lemmon's wallet only to have Lemmon turn the tables,
chase him, beat him to the ground, and get it back.
Alas, fresh from the creative freedom he'd enjoyed on
*The Lords of Flatbush,* Sylvester improvised, "Are
you nuts?" when accosted by Lemmon. A hush fell
over the set, and the script girl hurried over, quickly
and sternly informing him, "Excuse me, but you can't
ad-lib in Neil Simon!"

The chastisement rolled off his back, since Sylvester
regarded the part as one that required "great wind"
and "not too much acting talent." But it was the last
film work he could muster in the Big Apple.

Despondent, Sylvester was forced to admit that
maybe it wasn't such a good idea to stay in New York.
He was no longer considering giving up acting, but
after watching his costars from *The Lords of Flatbush*
go to Hollywood and land jobs, he talked it over with
Sasha and they decided to do the same.

At the time, they had nearly $4000 in the bank.
Using $40 of that, they bought a ten-year-old Oldsmo-

bile and drove west, accompanied by their bull mastiff, Butkus, named after the great Chicago Bears linebacker Dick Butkus. "The car," Sylvester swears, "exploded just as we reached Sunset and Vine." But they made it, and after Sylvester paused to buy "a 32-cent pair of sunglasses," they went looking for an apartment. They ended up taking a dilapidated room on Hollywood Boulevard which cost them $215 a month, and Sylvester immediately began making the rounds. He later joked that after hitting Hollywood, though he still didn't have any money, at least he got a tan.

Thanks to his credentials, slim as they were, Sylvester managed to get an agent and tried out for countless pictures, among them *Dog Day Afternoon, Rollerball, Serpico,* and *The Godfather, Part II.* Unhappily, all he did was try out. A particularly bitter loss was the film *Stay Hungry.* Set in a health club, *Stay Hungry* starred Sally Field as a promiscuous receptionist, and Sylvester went to the audition convinced that he was a shoo-in for the part of a bodybuilder. Much to his disappointment, he lost the role to another movie newcomer, the imposing Arnold Schwarzenegger.

For the first year, his work was limited to bit parts as thugs in TV shows like "Kojak" and "Police Story." He tried not to be dejected and constantly reminded himself that he could "take it or leave it. I always had my writing. I was independent." And write he did, waking at around 6:30 each and every morning and working on one screenplay or another. His major work during this period was a project set in the forties called *Hell's Kitchen,* the story of three brothers who try to use boxing as a means of escaping their poverty. *Hell's Kitchen* was Sylvester's first big-screen sale, in April of 1975, and for the first time in his life he was actually solvent. The buyers were producers John Roach and Ron Suppa, who paid Sylvester $21,500 for the script after previously having given him $2000 for an option (the exclusive right to buy the script outright within a certain period, usually six months) and $1500 for some rewriting. Given that he'd only made $1400 from acting that year, the sale was like manna. (A year later, it was manna that would give Sylvester a serious case of heartburn.)

Though the kind of fame Winkler had found in Southern California eluded Sylvester, being in Hollywood did have one advantage: he managed to keep working. Movies are ground out like sausage, and from 1974 through early 1975, Sylvester was able to get himself into a number of vacheburgers. He played a hoodlum who tussled briefly with Robert Mitchum in *Farewell My Lovely* and, down to his last $4, won the pivotal role of Frank "The Enforcer" Nitti, the bodyguard of Al Capone (Ben Gazzara), in the low-budget gangster thriller *Capone*. As it turned out, the part of Nitti was considerably different from the mindless hoods he'd played in other films. This time around he was a thinking-man's thug. As Nitti himself puts it after betraying Capone to the Feds, "Capone was as stupid as the ass end of a horse. He was so busy pumping bullets into the guy across the street that he forgot something. The guy you really got to watch out for is the bozo standing on the same ladder you are."

*Capone* was a typical gangster film, but there was

nothing typical about the other film Sylvester made during this period, the wonderfully glib, satirical *Death Race 2000*. Produced on a bigger budget than any Stallone picture to date, this futuristic thriller was the story of five drivers dashing cross-country in the challenging Trans Continental Road Race. But there's a twist to this race: not only do the drivers try to finish first, but they also score points for every pedestrian they run over and kill. (Old people are the choicest prey, earning seventy points apiece.) Sylvester played the nasty but natty Machine Gun Joe Viterbo ("loved by thousands, hated by millions"); his opponents were Matilda the Hun, Calamity Jane, Nero the Hero, and David Carradine as Frankenstein, so called because he was believed to have been cobbled together by Swiss mechanics. In the end, only Sylvester and Carradine make it into the home stretch, Sylvester perishing when Carradine's explosive artificial hand (a so-called hand grenade) is tossed into his car.

Once more of historical–pugilistic interest, *Death Race 2000* contains the only scene in which Sylvester has ever decked a woman, giving his girlfriend a pistonlike slug when she talks back to him. While it's impossible to predict what Rambo will do in the future, it's fair to say that this will remain an isolated incident in the Stallone repertoire. The picture also boasts a fist fight between Sylvester and Carradine, with the slender Carradine winning handily.

Because of its violence and excellent stunt work, *Death Race 2000* brought more than $5 million to its producers. Sylvester, who had once again worked for a relative pittance, saw none of that money.

Sylvester and Sasha had been married on December 28, 1974. Though their finances were precarious at best, they knew even then that they wanted to conceive a child the following summer, when the astrological signs would be optimal. As Sylvester explains, "We wanted a Taurus sun with a Libra moon and Leo rising, with Mercury in its natural sign in Gemini, which gives an incredibly quick mind." In practical terms, this meant that Sylvester had to start earning some big dollars, or, come May of 1976, his newborn would be suckling on a radiator for heat.

As in his teenaged years, whether as a track star or as a renegade drama student at the University of Miami, Sylvester continued to do his best work when pressed. And it was in a state of quiet desperation, with Sylvester wanting a child and wanting more than ever to succeed, that a legend was born.

# Chapter

## Five

Sitting by his window overlooking Hollywood Boulevard, his seat "in the pancreas of Hollywood," and with a yellow pad on his lap, Sylvester remembered what his mother had predicted, that writing would be his salvation. He was coming to believe that and repeatedly told himself, "There's got to be a formula. There's got to be something." Something upbeat, something heroic. The kind of story he'd yearned to write in New York. He told himself, "Today, a man brings his family into a theater, and there he sees a man pull out a knife and cut a kid's head off, and a woman is being run over by a Ford Mustang. And the man in the theater says, 'Is there anybody here I can identify with? Is there anything here I want to see?' "

The answer was no, and Sylvester constantly admonished himself, "Go back to the basics! Nobody is asking me to win a Nobel Peace Prize or split the atom, to enlighten them or alter their philosophy. They want to be entertained, to break out of this anti-anti-anti-everything syndrome and move into a lighter, more optimistic rebuilding process. The death of the human spirit has gone too far."

Hollywood didn't agree with him, of course. Despite the fact that downbeat movies weren't doing well as a rule, the powers-that-be knew the right one could make a fortune, a film along the lines of *One Flew Over the Cuckoo's Nest, Dog Day Afternoon,* or *Lenny.*

But Sylvester followed his nose because, as he told *The New York Times,* if people wanted realism they would be cutting "holes in the livingroom wall and charging people $3 to sit and watch what's going on in the house." Sitting in his apartment, he firmly believed, as he later said in *Newsweek,* that "we are going to see the actor who will be a hero, the actor who will inspire confidence and imitativeness in his viewers. Positiveness!"

Naturally, in theory that was all well and good. The big question, the one that kept Sylvester awake at night and woke him up before dawn each morning, was how best to couch this positiveness, in what kind of story and with what kind of character. He knew he wanted someone who bucked the odds, feeling that people were fascinated with "the Rockefellers, the Gettys—not the sons, the originals. They were scrappers. They had a dream. They went out and conquered everything in their path." But so did Daniel Boone,

Hannibal, Galileo, and countless others. After writing scripts about nutty rock stars and eccentric actors, he just didn't know where to start.

Stymied, he went to the boxing match on March 15 not because he had it in mind to write about a boxer but primarily because he has always found "there's something about sweating that inspires me to write." And watching Wepner stand up to Ali, taking a serious punishment and trying to dish one out, he realized that a boxer would be the perfect hero for the mid-seventies.

He remembers walking out of the Wiltern Theater on the corner of Western and Wilshire Boulevard and saying to himself as he strolled home, "That's drama! Now the only thing I've got to do is get a character to that point and I've got my story."

Reaching that point was easier than he'd expected. Reflecting back on his own "stifled ambition and broken dreams," he quickly sketched in his mind a fictional boxer named Rocky Balboa, someone who loved fighting but didn't get the breaks, someone who "had drive and talent, but nobody noticed him," someone who paid his bills by working as the collector for a loanshark, yet was too sweet and good-natured to break the bones of people who didn't pay up.

The month during which he conceived the basic character was what Sylvester calls his inspiration stage. "Then," he continues, "I let it sit—the incubation stage." He smiles broadly. "After that came the verification stage, when I wrote the *Rocky* script." By that time, June of 1975, the character was so vivid in his mind that he was able to turn out the screenplay in an astonishing three and a half days.

Not long after he'd arrived in Hollywood, Sylvester had acquired the services of Larry Kubik as his agent. As it happens, Kubik was approached one day by a novice filmmaker named Gene Kirkwood. Kirkwood had been hired by veteran producers Irwin Winkler and Robert Chartoff to find new properties to produce, and he approached Kubik to see if he had anything interesting. Kubik suggested he talk to Sylvester, who he said was always brimming with ideas.

The two men got together, and the first thing they discussed was another project Sylvester had been kicking around, the story of a cab driver who runs for mayor of Philadelphia. Deciding that the idea had heart and humor but not a lot of energy, Sylvester reluctantly brought up *Rocky*.

The reason for his reluctance was that he hadn't really had a chance to polish the script. The screenplay he'd written in a fortnight was a very rough draft, and there were things he didn't like about it. For example, while it was still the story of a down-and-out fighter who is given a shot at the title when the scheduled contender hurts his hand, the characters in the first script were considerably different. Rocky's trainer, Mickey, was a racist, while Creed was a much older fighter, nearly forty. In the climax, Mickey's prejudice comes roaring to the surface as he screams at Rocky to kill his opponent, whom he has on the ropes. However, Mickey's slurs make Rocky furious, and, as Sylvester describes it, "Rocky lets himself get hit with a punch and then purposely falls flat on his face and loses the fight on a TKO." Retiring from the fight game, he takes the money from the bout and buys his girlfriend Adrian a pet shop.

Kirkwood agreed that having Rocky take a dive was a bad idea, but he loved the project to that point. At his suggestion, Sylvester went home and began working on a second draft. At first he toyed with the idea of having Rocky buck the odds and win the fight. Ultimately, he decided that that would make him just too unbelievable, destroying the all-important aspect of him being a "common man." Instead, he opted for the climax as it stands, in which he's beaten but becomes the first fighter to last a full fifteen rounds with Creed. As Rocky tells Adrian in the film, "If I can just go the distance, I'll know I'm not just another bum from the neighborhood." As Sylvester puts it, he kept reminding himself that winning wasn't the issue in *Rocky*. It was courage. "The antagonist is not the champion, Apollo Creed, it's fear of failure, of unrealized dreams." Keeping that in sharp focus, Sylvester was able to come up with the ending as it stands, producing a second draft in eighty-six hours, he and Sasha popping caffeine tablets while she typed up the finished copy.

Kirkwood liked the way Sylvester had resolved the story and, plugging in a few ideas of his own, worked with the screenwriter on a third draft. Then, in July, he brought the project to his colleagues.

Between them, Winkler and Chartoff had produced twenty-five pictures, among them Barbra Streisand's *Up the Sandbox, The New Centurions* starring George C. Scott, and the Oscar-winning *They Shoot Horses, Don't They?* The men knew a good human-interest story when they saw one and took Rocky to United Artists. The studio was equally impressed and, in

Winkler's words, made "an offer to buy it from Stallone." The sum they put forth was $75,000, and it was their plan, once they owned the script, to make the picture starring any one of a number of superstars. Among the names being tossed around were Ryan O'Neal, Burt Reynolds, Gene Hackman, Paul Newman, Robert Redford, and James Caan.

Sylvester was profoundly impressed by the offer, but he had a problem with it. Though he'd written the script specifically to put money in the bank, he realized that he didn't want anyone to play Rocky but himself. Collecting his nerve, he told the studio, "Thanks, but I can't sell it outright. I wrote it, and I have to do it." Perceiving this as a negotiating ploy, the studio promptly raised the offer another $50,000.

Sylvester says that thinking about the $125,000 on the table gave him "a monumental headache. I didn't know that much money existed." He adds that Chartoff and Winkler kept reminding him that the movie had very little chance of being financed unless it had a big-name star. But Sylvester couldn't bring himself to bow out, saying with just a touch of melodrama, "The story was about not selling out, about having faith in yourself, about going the distance as a million-to-one shot." He repeated that he simply had to star in the film, at which point the buying price was upped to a mouth-watering $350,000.

That one really got Sylvester's attention, and he had a heart-to-heart talk with Sasha. By this time she was pregnant, they were still living in their ramshackle Hollywood apartment—though for how much longer they weren't sure, Sylvester noting that the landlord "wanted to see me on the curb"—and, as an actor, Sylvester realized he was "about as marketable as tear gas." But he also knew that he would "rather bury the script in the backyard and let the caterpillars play Rocky" than give it to someone else, and not just because he had put his heart and pieces of his life into the script. His reasons were more practical than that: he knew that "this part was the only shot I'd ever get" at a truly great, tailor-made starring role.

Discussing it with Sylvester over their rickety kitchen table, Sasha tried to minimize the offer.

"What does $350,000 look like?" she asked.

Staring at his lap, Sylvester replied, "I don't know."

"I don't know either," she said quickly, "so I guess I wouldn't really miss it."

Sylvester looked up. "But if I *don't* sell it, how do you feel about having to go to the backyard and eat grass?"

Her reply: "I'd sooner move to a trailer in the middle of a swamp than for you to sell *Rocky*."

Sylvester called the producers and as politely as he knew how told them that he wouldn't give them the script "for a million dollars" unless he was the star.

Chartoff, Winkler, and Kirkwood were disappointed. Yet they felt the project still might get backing if they could come up with a reasonable budget. They slashed away at salaries, worked out a shooting schedule that was bare-bones minimum, and came away with an extremely modest budget of $1,750,000. Their hopes high, they sat down with United Artists, which at first still resisted having Sylvester as the star. He wasn't surprised. The first time he'd met with the studio people, he says, "they thought I was a hat-check girl and handed me their coats when they came in to talk."

The studio's biggest problem with Sylvester was that they didn't know if he had the charisma to be a leading man. In fact, they weren't even sure they liked him as a boxer.

"They said I didn't have the stature," Sylvester told Lawrence Linderman of *Playboy*. "I told them, 'I'm bigger than Rocky Marciano was in his prime. I have a 73-inch reach, and he had a 68-inch reach. His biceps were 14 inches, and mine are 17 inches." He added, "I hate to tell you what I thought they might want to measure next."

Conceding that Sylvester had a point, United Artists agreed to give the actor a shot, but only under four conditions. First, they wanted the option to replace him early on if they didn't like his performance; second, the budget would have to be trimmed to an even $1 million; third, Chartoff and Winkler would have to agree to pay for any budget overruns out of their own pockets; and, fourth, they wanted the arrogant Apollo Creed changed so that he was less like Muhammad Ali, lest the champ or his fans take offense.

Obviously, it wasn't quite the deal the producers were hoping to make. Nonetheless, they looked into the finances to see if the film could be made for such a ridiculously small amount of money. For while it was true that pictures such as *The Lords of Flatbush* were made for less than half the sum United Artists was offering, that film was nonunion, had taken two years to shoot, and also *looked* cheap, with bad lighting and worse sound. *Rocky* had to be a top-drawer package all around.

Salaries were reduced further in exchange for the participants' owning a percentage of the film. Chartoff and Winkler agreed to take nothing up front, and Sylvester was told he'd receive no more than $20,000 for his services as screenwriter. He would also have to work for scale as star. He agreed, and while he didn't tell the producers, he later admitted, "I was willing to do the picture for $1.50 a day and a hot lunch, just for the chance."

Relative unknowns and nonactors were penciled in for the supporting roles, and even Sylvester's family was advised they'd have to take parts in order to help round out the cast. In the finished film, Frank Sr. can be seen as the fight timekeeper, Frank Jr. is on display as a streetcorner singer—he also wrote the music and lyrics for the film's "Take Me Back"—and even Butkus made a guest appearance. Sylvester was disappointed to note, however, that the dog "had problems with his dialogue." As for Sasha, though her bit part ended up on the cutting-room floor, she saved the unit money by taking many of the photographs, while Sylvester did multiple duty by dubbing four voices heard in bar scenes, on televisions, and elsewhere in the background, saving the producers $200.

Costs were reduced further by making plans to use real locations wherever possible, thus cutting down on the number of sets that would have to be constructed. This included the gym and the frozen meat chamber where Rocky works out by punching sides of beef. File footage of crowds from actual fights would be used for the title bout, the size of the crew would be kept down, and extravagances, both personal and creative, would be nonexistent. For instance, in the script there was a scene in which Rocky and Adrian visit a crowded skating rink. To save money on extras, the setting was changed to a closed rink (which, in turn, enabled Sylvester to write and perform a touching scene in which Rocky haggles for time in the rink with a sour-faced attendant). Moreover, the large float on which Apollo Creed enters the arena for the title bout was filmed from only one side so that the other side didn't have to be painted.

Perhaps the most extraordinary adjustment of all was in the climactic scene. Instead of hiring extras to loft Rocky onto their shoulders and carry him from the ring, Sylvester conceived of having him walk off alone to be with Adrian. Not only did it save the filmmakers money but, in terms of the film itself, it also made the budding romance between Rocky and Adrian that much more moving.

The budget came down dramatically, but it was still necessary to find a top director who would work for a ridiculously low sum and a percentage of the profits. The producers approached five directors, and all of them turned down the picture because they either didn't like the script, didn't think Sylvester was right for the part, or simply didn't want to take less than their normal fee. Finally, John G. Avildsen of *Joe* and *Save the Tiger* fame read the script, fell in love with it, and agreed to direct at only half his usual fee of $100,000.

Though he was amazed that they'd managed to do

so much belt tightening, Winkler was still understandably anxious. "I still can't believe I mortgaged my house to put up the $50,000 completion bond for *Rocky*," he said when the picture was finished. But the atmosphere surrounding the picture had become infused with a Rocky-like do-or-die mentality, and people did things they wouldn't ordinarily have done. Even Sylvester's representatives managed the impossible when it came to dealing with United Artists, especially the stipulation that the studio be allowed to pull the plug on him if they didn't like the work he was doing.

The deal hammered out for Sylvester by attorney Jake Bloom and his associates stated that if United Artists was displeased with Sylvester, they could replace him, but only after seventeen days, the halfway point of the shooting schedule. Bloom and his people further insisted that the Philadelphia locations be filmed first. That was a key concession to wrest from the studio, for it was the most expensive part of the shoot. With more than half the money spent and the picture half done, chances were good that the studio wouldn't exercise their option to replace Sylvester, even if they weren't entirely satisfied. It was a masterpiece of negotiating on Bloom's part, and, not surprisingly, his firm continues to represent Sylvester to this day.

Regarding United Artists' last demand, that Apollo be made less like Ali, Sylvester took care of that by making him Jamaican. The studio was satisfied, and, as soon as he sat down on the plane for the flight to Philadelphia, Sylvester flipped down the meal tray, broke out the script, and changed it back to the way he'd originally written it.

Everything was in readiness, the impossible had been accomplished, and now only one thing concerned Sylvester: that after all the grandstanding he'd done to get the part of Rocky Balboa, he not bungle the job. He says he was constantly haunted by fighter Rocky Graziano's famous saying, "Fighting is the only racket where you're almost guaranteed to end up as a bum," and hoped that didn't hold true for movies about fighters.

With a bittersweet tone to his voice, he remembers how anxious he was before filming actually got underway. Then, suddenly, it all came together for him.

"I couldn't believe it was actually happening," he begins. "The first day of shooting, it was 19 degrees, miserable. We were in Philadelphia. And when I walked out of the trailer at 4:30 in the morning, I paused in front of the mirror. And I said, 'Sylvester, for twenty-nine years you've been talking a great game. Now either you prove it, or you're dead.' I knew when I looked in that mirror that this man was either going to walk out a hero or a totally disgraced wretch who had been living a life of illusions—sad, gas-filled dreams." The bittersweet tone hardens. "But then I walked out of the trailer and my foot hit the pavement and the cold tightened my face. And I knew," he smiles, "that it was in the bag."

# Chapter

## Six

Though it had been a long, emotionally draining haul to get *Rocky* into production, Sylvester's battle didn't end when the actor and his creation merged that morning in Philadelphia. In many ways, the toughest part was about to begin.

He had always been in good physical condition, but to play a championship boxer required more than a well-developed torso. He had to convince audiences that a lifetime of boxing skills and reflexes were second nature to him, he had to be fit enough to endure the blows he would be taking in the staging of the championship bout, and, from an acting point of view, he had to learn to think like a boxer.

The last objective was the easiest. Sylvester actually

undertook to slow his mind down, going on a diet designed to "severely change my intelligence level, which it did. I went on a strict shrimp and shellfish diet, with no carbohydrates whatsoever, and eventually my intelligence level dropped to the point where I'd want to listen to country and western music, which is really bizarre for me." He adds that he went around poking at his nose and mumbling to himself, staying in character around the clock.

Getting ready physically wasn't quite so easy, especially when it came to toughening up for the bout with Apollo.

Delivering the blows as Apollo Creed was a man who stood 4 inches taller than Sylvester, 6-foot 2-inch, twenty-eight-year-old Carl Weathers, a former football player with the Oakland Raiders.

Weathers recalls that his first meeting with his costar was anything but auspicious. Auditioning for the part, he was asked to box a bit with Sylvester, who he thought was merely the writer of the movie. Weathers and Sylvester sparred, and at one point the burly ex-athlete landed a particularly strong blow on his partner's chin. Sylvester stepped back and said good-naturedly, "Hey, remember, it's only an audition."

Annoyed at being told to hold back when he really wanted to show the producers what he could do, Weathers complained, "You know, I should have the *real* actor here to fight."

Grinning, Sylvester said, "I *am* the real actor."

Realizing he'd implied that the star of *Rocky* was a wimp, Weathers assumed he'd blown the role. But despite the awkward beginning, Weathers did well in the test bout and superbly in the reading, and he was named to play Apollo Creed. Not surprisingly, the two men had a healthy rivalry during the grueling five-month training period that followed.

Sylvester's daily regimen was not unlike Rocky's. He would sleep an hour later than the contender— Sylvester didn't get up until dawn—at which point he would go to the bathroom mirror and say to himself, "Here we are. It's another day. You're gonna do better than yesterday." After gulping down 44 of the 113 vitamin pills he would take each day, Sylvester would drive to the Malibu beaches and run for five miles, then commute twenty miles to a gym in Chatsworth. While Sylvester would have preferred to spare himself the drive, the cost of facilities in Hollywood was prohibitive. In Chatsworth he worked out with Jimmy Gambina, a former fight trainer who ended up acting in the film and serving as its technical director as well.

Sylvester's workouts included doing countless pushups, having a medicine ball heaved at his stomach, and, of course, learning to box like Rocky, whom Sylvester describes as "a flatfooted steam engine who took ten punches to give one." And each night he would come home not only exhausted but bruised. He remembers that sparring was particularly difficult, since he wasn't going up against actors or stunt people but real boxers who "hit me so hard sometimes I couldn't even remember my phone number. Boxing is just about the only sport where you can come out mentally inferior to when you went in. You don't get wiser; you lose your marbles."

But tired as he was, Sylvester's training didn't stop

when he dragged himself home. After his shrimp dinner, he'd flop down in a chair and "study a lot of fight films and borrow ideas for *Rocky*." Inspired by what he saw, he'd spend time with the punching bag he'd hung in the living room, following that with long stretches of shadow boxing—fighting imaginary opponents all around the apartment, jumping, jabbing, and panting until the only way Sasha could bring him back to reality was by literally ringing the bell on the oven and shouting "Time!" Sasha declares, "I went through *horrors*. He trained as if he really were preparing for a championship."

Which, in Sylvester's mind, is exactly what he was doing, and by the time he was finished training, Sylvester was convinced that he could last six rounds in the ring with a bona fide contender for the heavyweight title.

As the February 1976 start for the picture neared, Sylvester was confident enough about his boxing ability to turn to one of the most crucial aspects of the film, Rocky's climactic battle with Apollo Creed. Putting it into the script, he laughs, had been easy: he'd simply written "fourteen pages of left, right, right, left, left, hook." Now it was time to work it all out in the ring, a job that fell primarily to Sylvester. He accepted this responsibility not because of ego but because he was the only one associated with the picture who understood both film and fighting; staging it himself was the only way to achieve what he described as "poetry with perspiration."

After their daily workouts, Sylvester and Weathers would get together and block out the action, both actors justifiably proud of the fact that what looks

utterly haphazard and impromptu on the screen was as
carefully choreographed as a ballet ("a ballet of the
grotesque," as Sylvester likes to call it).

The men started by trying out the most impressive
moves they'd seen in the fight films of the best and
most visual fighters, predominantly Rocky Marciano,
Joe Louis, Sonny Liston, and Muhammad Ali. Then
they would tailor these moves to their own characters,
Weathers paying particular attention to Ali since
Creed was patterned after the heavyweight champ.
Then they would discard what wasn't comfortable,
invent their own exchanges, and study super-8 mm
films that Avildsen took of their bouts to see what was
exciting cinematically and what was not. Making the
task doubly difficult was that the men naturally didn't
want to hurt themselves, so they had to remember to
roll with each other's punches. Months after the filming was completed, Sylvester noted, "My neck is still
stiff from snapping back from those jabs of Carl
Weathers. He got so fast that when I was editing the
film I'd find a punch in just one frame. There are 24
frames a second, so that was $1/24$th of a second and the
punch was gone." (He also complained that his father
had kept forgetting to ring the bell, so he and Weathers
would keep on slugging at each other while Sylvester
snarled, "Bell . . . *bell!*" from the corner of his
mouth.)

By February, everything was ready. The cast and
crew flew to Philadelphia to shoot all the exteriors, and
twenty-eight days and $960,000 later, *Rocky* was in the
can. ("Twenty-eight days," Sylvester deadpans, "the
gestation time for a water bug.")

It had been a miraculously fast and easy shoot,

made smoother by the professionalism of the stars, which included Talia Shire as Adrian, Burt Young as her opportunistic brother Paulie, and Burgess Meredith as the crusty, nonracist Mickey. Not that there weren't problems. The board of health came by and closed the commissary—which, because of the low budget, was not as sanitary as it should have been—and the actors tended to get a little cranky because they spent their days in what Shire describes as "stalls instead of trailers." But when the cameras rolled, the hardships were forgotten, and everyone went for the acting gold.

Shire had previously costarred in *The Godfather* and *The Godfather, Part II* (for which she was nominated for an Oscar), and Sylvester credits her professionalism and empathy with having made his job much easier. In her brief career, she not only had seen other young actors cope with the pressure of having an entire movie on their back—notably newcomers Al Pacino and James Caan in *The Godfather*—but, as the sister of director Francis Ford Coppola, she had a unique perspective on the industry as a whole. Some advice she gave Sylvester early on, while they were sitting in his trailer, helped him keep *Rocky* in perspective. "A star," she said, "is nothing but a hanging ball of gas." If *Rocky* were a hit, that would be fine, she told him. Otherwise, he was still an actor and, one way or another, he would manage to find work.

Notwithstanding the good sense of that, Sylvester still couldn't rid himself entirely of his do-or-die mentality. He fretted over every aspect of the film to a degree that often annoyed the cast and crew. He voiced strong opinions about what kind of glasses

Adrian should wear and what kind of hairdo she should have. He argued with veteran actor Meredith over how they should play their scenes together. Later, when the filming was completed, he fought with Avildsen about which scenes to leave in and which to cut. (*Newsweek* reported that "to settle one disagreement, Stallone picked up the shorter Avildsen, according to one account, and slammed him against the door.")

Sylvester freely admits that he sometimes overstepped his authority and managed to make "a total enemy of everyone on the set"—so much so that some of the crew members who worked on the film insisted that their names be removed from the credits. But in Sylvester's defense, it wasn't a matter of the lead throwing his weight around or his paranoia getting the best of him. He was both the author of and the authority on the script and as such had very strong ideas about the characters and situations. Nor did he feel any compunction about expressing these, often bluntly and at high volume; he knew they had to make the movie fast and that debate was anathema to speed.

One of the stars who ultimately became his defender was Burt Young. "That kid Sylvester, he was *tough*," Young agreed. But he added, "It's a hard thing to walk into a film where it's on your back like that. And the son of a gun fooled me! I have nothing but respect for the kid."

For his part, Avildsen allows that the creative dividends of having Sylvester around outweighed the drawbacks. "We were able to shape the story," he acknowledges, "to bring out things just because the

actor and the writer were there on the scene in one
person, someone who understood what a scene
needed. We were able to bounce ideas off one another.
And Stallone showed himself to have a deep sensitivity for the part he was playing."

Given the physical nature of the film, one thing that
surprised everyone, Sylvester included, was that there
were few injuries. Sylvester pulled leg tendons while
running on the concrete streets of Philadelphia ("They
had to take me home in a wheelbarrow," he winces),
but, as opposed to future Rocky films when overexer-
tion or the fights themselves would put the star in the
hospital, this first tilt with Apollo Creed went relatively smoothly. All Sylvester suffered was a cracked
hip bone, for which he wasn't even hospitalized. The
bout was shot at the Los Angeles Sports Arena, with
four cameras trained on the action, one of which was
hand carried in the ring for close-ups. Apart from
Sylvester's hip injury, the only time the fight was
stopped was when it was necessary for makeup artist
Mike Westmore to apply heavier bruises, deeper cuts,
or thickening streams of blood.

United Artists was happy with the finished film and
made every effort to ensure that people within the
industry understood that it was not "just" a boxing
picture. This was stressed to the point of overkill in a
circular sent to theater owners, journalists, and others
who could help make or break the picture. The bro-
chure read:

For every kid who's ever dreamed of growing up to
be President or to walk on the moon or become

champion of the world, for every girl who's ever
dreamed of being Garbo or Monroe, for everyone
who's ever had a dream, once in a rare lifetime,
against impossible odds, you just might get a shot at
it. *Rocky* is the story of that dream and a man
whose whole life was a million-to-one shot.

The one picture printed with the copy showed Rocky
and Adrian embracing without a boxing glove or heavy
bag in view.

It was a soapy, meandering pitch, but United Artists
knew that no boxing film had ever made more than a
minimal profit, and they wanted to play that aspect
down as much as possible. The studio's outside hope
was that the picture could take in about $4 or $5
million. Since a movie has to gross its cost plus
approximately 150 percent before it shows a profit—
the additional monies representing the cost of prints
and advertising, which are not computed as part of the
budget—United Artists felt they could look forward to
a profit of a million or two.

Much to United Artists' surprise, when *Rocky*
opened late in 1976, it was a phenomenon unlike any
Hollywood had seen for quite some time. On the one
hand, of course, it represented a financial windfall for
everyone concerned. The studio netted $55,925,000,
of which Sylvester was entitled to 1 percent as writer
and 2 percent as actor. His reward for sticking to his
guns was nearly $2 million, with more to come from
subsidiary sales to cable, cassette, and network television. (By July of 1977, however, he still hadn't been
paid a penny—"It's lost in transit," he said cyni-

cally—and had to threaten legal action to collect. His agent dramatically delivered it to him in cash, via armored truck, while he was on the set of his next movie.) Although he was reported to be slightly bitter about the fact that the producers earned several times that sum from his creative sweat, he had to admit he wasn't doing badly for someone whose car had to be towed from Sunset Boulevard not long before. In fact, with his first profit-sharing check, Sylvester finally got rid of the battered Oldsmobile in which he and Sasha had driven cross-country and treated himself to a stunning, off-white, leather-upholstered Mercedes 450 SE.

The box office returns were thrilling, not only to Sylvester but to Burgess Meredith who cheered, "After appearing in over 120 films, *Rocky* was my very first smash hit!" However, making the success even sweeter was the fact that *Rocky* was also an artistic success. It earned accolades from most critics, as well as ten Oscar nominations. Of particular significance regarding the Oscars were Sylvester's nominations for Best Actor and Best Screenplay. Only twice before in the history of the Academy Awards had one person been nominated in those categories for a single film. Those nominees were Charlie Chaplin and Orson Welles—not bad company at all. And while Sylvester himself failed to take home an award, *Rocky* won the Oscar for Best Picture of the Year, and Avildsen took the honors as Best Director. The movie also won for best editing, though the popular theme song, "Gonna Fly Now," incomprehensibly lost to "Evergreen," the love theme from *A Star Is Born*.

Regarding Avildsen's Oscar, the director delights in recounting the bizarre manner in which he first learned of his nomination. He was in the office of Robert Stigwood, the producer of *Saturday Night Fever,* a film Avildsen was slated to direct. Avildsen remembers, "I wanted to make a very uplifting, positive, reassuring statement as in *Rocky;* he seemed to want something more like *Taxi Driver.* I'm arguing that my idea could really work, and he's shaking his head no when the phone rings. He says, 'That was your assistant. Congratulations: *Rocky* just got ten nominations and you're up for Best Director. But I still think your idea stinks.'" Avildsen was fired shortly before taking home the statuette.

The Oscar nominations notwithstanding, the proudest critical reception Sylvester received was on the day he flew his mother out for an advance showing of *Rocky.* After the picture had begun unspooling, Sylvester impulsively jumped onto the small stage and yelled, "Hey Ma—I made it! I *made* it, Ma!" Alone in the private screening room, Jacqueline wept. . . .

When the dust unexpectedly swirled up by the honors and profits began to settle, what proved most incredible of all about the film was its cultural impact. People started running to gyms to build themselves up, and "real" men displayed their fortitude by eating raw eggs the way Rocky does in the film. (Sylvester quipped, "After about three weeks they'll come to their senses and return to the yoga-and-yogurt set.") There were even debates in the press about what was realistic and what was not in the boxing scenes. For instance, boxer Harold Weston complained that having Mickey tie Rocky's legs together to improve his

balance was "a whole lot of jive," and trainer Gil
Clancy said the most realistic thing about the film was
"the way the gyms are." Moreover, every time a star
was spotted at the film, he or she was asked for an
opinion. Al Pacino refused to tender one, but *The
Village Voice* dutifully reported that "he muttered
'Jesus Christ' during Sylvester Stallone's incredible
exercise scene [and] applauded after the big fight
sequence."

Naturally, everyone involved with the film had his
or her own opinions about exactly why *Rocky* was so
appealing. Avildsen declared, "Boxing is just about
the dumbest thing in the world, but this is a sensitive
story about a man who is not exactly what you would
call a winner." He said the basis of the film's appeal
was that people had no trouble identifying with Rocky.
Coproducer Winkler agreed, stating, "This film is not
just a prize-fight drama. It's in the tradition of the
classic Frank Capra films, about a good man with
courage and spirit who overcomes all obstacles." As
for Frank Capra himself, all the seventy-nine-year-old
director of such classics as *Mr. Smith Goes to Washington* and *It's a Wonderful Life* could say was, "Boy,
that's a picture I wish I made."

Not surprisingly, Sylvester himself didn't believe
that the boxing was either dumb or peripheral. While
agreeing that everyone liked the big-hearted Rocky, he
says that boxing films are popular "because we all
know what it's like to wanna hit somebody. You can
relate to it because you've wanted to punch someone
in the face, like maybe your boss, or your brother or
sister, or even the person you're married to."

Like the popularity of *Rocky*, the popularity of

Sylvester Stallone was attributed to a mix of qualities. Gene Kirkwood declaimed, "He's the first leading man to come along that's a *man* and yet he's still like a little gentle kitten in the film." *Newsweek* gushed that he was a genuine original, "innocently sexy," that "his acting is unaffected [and] he conveys deep vulnerability but without baroque psychological nuances." New York's *Daily News* agreed, describing Sylvester's performance as "a mixture of boyish intensity, lusty sensuality, and cheerful innocence." United Artists executive Mike Medavoy went even further, pulling out the stops and exclaiming, "I can't recall such excitement about a new movie and a new star since maybe *Giant* and James Dean."

Unfortunately for Sylvester, success as an actor and success as a person are two different things. In the aftermath of *Rocky,* he learned the hard way that it required a special kind of talent to manage them both.

# Chapter

## Seven

Sylvester was thrilled by the acclaim and by the simple courtesies everyone he met stumbled over themselves to extend, from superb service at the gas station to immediate seating at crowded restaurants. However, as much as he enjoyed the star treatment, he was still slightly cynical as he thought back to how he had struggled for so many years without recognition. "It's funny," he said, "but now there's this great herd of people who are coming forth and saying, 'I like you.' It happened to Rocky too. I feel like saying to them, 'Where were you when I was living in Hotel Barf, eating hot and cold running disease?' They say, 'Oh, we were holding it back, Sly, because we didn't want you to get a swelled head.'"

But bitterness was only a brief phase in the wake of the *Rocky* phenomenon. When he sifted through the flood of emotions he was feeling, what was really gratifying about the whole experience was that he'd achieved the goal that had taken root on the New York subway years before. He had given people a hero, and, as a bonus, they were taking hope from his own Cinderella story.

"You know," he said earnestly, "if nothing else comes out of that film in the way of awards and accolades, it will still show that an unknown quantity, a totally unmarketable person, can produce a diamond in the rough, a gem. And there's a lot more people like me out there too." And his message to those people, the moral that both he and Rocky had learned, was simple: "If you lead with your heart, it will carry you much farther than your brains will. If you have heart, you can succeed in anything."

Meanwhile, the post-*Rocky* highs continued. Getting out of his Hollywood apartment was one. Sylvester moved his family into a four-bedroom Coldwater Canyon mansion previously owned by comedian Ernie Kovacs, a quirky house complete with phony cobwebs in the wine cellar and rhinoceros-head fountain-outside. The move had come none too soon, as their Hollywood apartment had become inordinately cramped. In addition to boxing paraphernalia, which Sylvester kept around even after filming had been completed, the Stallones had been joined in May of 1976 by son Sage Moonblood, called Sage because it meant "wisdom" and Moonblood after one of Sylvester's screenwriting pseudonyms, Q. Moonblood.

(He'd concocted that name because the words reminded him of Poe.)

Professionally, roles were offered to him left and right, not the least of which was the chance to play Superman in the $30 million film costarring Marlon Brando. ("I hope he doesn't think I do a cheap imitation of him because of the undershirt," Sylvester worried. "Italians *do* wear undershirts.") He eventually decided against that one, as well as virtually everything else he was offered, most of which were "gangster movies or more fight films, real lame stuff." What he was looking for, he said, was "a real test of acting, something that would be kind of important." He said he wanted to do something that would cause people to say, "Yeah, all right, he's not a boxer, he can act a little."

Because Sylvester was a hot property, not only was he sent stacks of screenplays but he also had a relatively easy time selling scripts of his own. One of them, *The Bodyguard,* was a particular favorite, the story of a man who is assigned to protect the wife and child of a millionaire. When they are murdered, the bodyguard takes it upon himself to hunt down their killers. That one was picked up by Universal for a rather substantial $200,000, reportedly with the contractual provision that a Porsche Turbo Carrera which Sylvester had written into the script be turned over to him when filming was completed. While it has yet to be filmed, Sylvester hopes to make it in the near future.

But there were lows as well. They were oppressive not only because Sylvester had had enough heartache but because he had been expecting *more* happiness from his achievements. As Talia Shire accurately observed, "Francis was an innocent when he first succeeded, and so is Sly."

The first disappointment came immediately after *Rocky* took off and a lawsuit was filed charging, rather incredibly, that Sylvester had ripped himself off. The plaintiffs were John Roach and Ron Suppa, who claimed that *Rocky* was strongly reminiscent of *Hell's Kitchen,* such as in the fact that one of the brothers, Victor, was a boxer, that a working title for the script had been *Italian Stallion,* which was Rocky's nom de guerre in the film; and that overall the "theme, mood, format, characters, and structure" of the two pieces were similar enough to warrant legal relief.

Sylvester was flabbergasted. "How can it be plagiarism? They're both my scripts!" Fresh from having played a man who lived by his fists, he said disgustedly, "You know, you don't meet a guy in an alley anymore. Now it's, 'My lawyer will notify you. I'll meet you in court.'"

He didn't like it, but the lawsuit paled in the face of other eye openers—the press, for example. Everywhere he turned he found himself pursued by a reporter or photographer, and the novelty quickly faded. To be sure, when he'd finished *Rocky* and wanted to promote it, he talked to just about anyone with a tape recorder. But that was over and done with, and he couldn't understand why everyone didn't just go away and come back when he started his next picture. By the end of 1976, if Sylvester walked out to the curb to get the newspaper, someone was there to take his picture. If he and Sasha went to a restaurant, the morning papers had the photographs along with a rundown of what they'd eaten. He complained to columnist Earl Wilson that he couldn't go anywhere without "thirty guys jumping up and shooting" him, and he actually took to using a variety of tactics to discourage them, including cutting eyeholes in a paper bag and wearing it over his head. Even that wasn't foolproof, since the shutterbugs took to following him around until he took the bag off. Sylvester theorized, "The only way I could walk around unnoticed would be by using a Groucho Marx mask."

As nettlesome as the journalists could be, however, the fans proved even more unnerving to him. The public had indeed let Rocky into their hearts, and they just wouldn't let go. "At first," he confided to critic Roger Ebert, "the crowds were fun. I signed a lot of autographs." The problem, he went on, was that "people want more than you can give them. At first they want to touch. Then they want to grab. I'm not a person anymore; I'm someone to be challenged and taunted."

Men greeted him not with a handshake but with a bodypunch, and women were worse because they were totally unpredictable. He talks with a mixture of awe and consternation about a photograph that was taken at this time. "It's the strangest thing. I'm signing autographs and this young girl is reaching out to touch me, and she has the most frightening look on her face, as if this instant is transcendent for her. She isn't touching me; she's touching Rocky, an unreal person." Another time a woman went to the opposite extreme, hitting him hard on the jaw. "I asked her why she'd done a thing like that, and she said, 'Because you got what I want!'" She wanted to destroy what she couldn't have. While this incident occurred more than three years before Mark Chapman killed John Lennon, Sylvester began to worry about the physical danger of celebrity. He confided, "One of these days some nutso might have a knife." By June of 1977, on the set of his new film *F.I.S.T.*, he admitted, "I'm getting paranoid. As soon as they touch me, my hand balls up into a fist."

Just how volatile Sylvester had become is clear from what happened one day when he was involved in a car accident. Another driver ran into him, and Sylvester got out, complaining, "Don't you think you should apologize?"

Instead of agreeing, the other driver told him flat out, "Go to hell."

Steamed, Sylvester shot back, "Hey, I could've had my kid in the car!"

Unmoved, the driver repeated, "Go to hell!"

Having had enough of selfish people, Sylvester saw no recourse but to "stretch him," which he did with "a wide, arcing left." The actor ended up having to settle with the man for $15,000 and decided that thereafter it would be safer, not to mention less expensive, if he simply kept his distance from the public.

In time, Sylvester's concern became so acute that when he moved into his second home, a sprawling estate in the Pacific Palisades, he erected a high brick wall around the house, hired an armed guard to answer the door, and installed seven closed-circuit TV cameras which transmitted a 360-degree exterior view to screens in the kitchen.

In light of these and other developments, the aftermath of *Rocky* was even harder on Sasha than it was on Sylvester. It wasn't only concern for their security or having to share her husband with the public; there was also a dramatic change in the way they related to each other. And it weighed much more heavily on her than on Sylvester.

"From the very first, we were a working couple," she explains. "All my ambition, all my energy, went into working with him. The baby and *Rocky* changed that. I was at home with the baby; he was at the studio editing. We were apart for the first time. He'd come home and try to share his day with me, but it was hard for both of us."

What made it especially difficult was that, since Sylvester was having such a difficult time choosing his next film, he jumped feet first into the difficult task of turning his screenplay for *Hell's Kitchen* into a novel. The Roach–Suppa lawsuit was more or less defused when Sylvester changed the story's protagonist from a boxer to a wrestler, played up the forties ambience, and made sundry other alterations. The picture, now known as *Paradise Alley*, was placed on Universal's production slate, and the novel was signed up by the studio's publishing arm. Sylvester was given an office at the studio where he could work on the novel, and, says Sasha, "not being involved in it" made her "very restless. I started asking if I could come to the studio, but he just said it was boring there. I would say, 'Why don't we just be bored together like we used to be?' " But Sylvester would "come home, eat dinner, and fall asleep without saying more than four words," and the two just drifted apart.

Making matters worse was the way he squelched her
when she tried to turn her interest in photography into
a vocation. She'd had a great time working on *Rocky*
and taking the photos of Sylvester that appeared in the
September 1978 *Playboy* interview. Sasha says she
"wanted to become a professional, but Sly did not
want me to work. If I took on assignments, he knew
that I would not always be available to him." She gave
it up to keep the peace, turning to other hobbies such
as decorating the house and scuba diving. But the
seeds of resentment had been planted, and they would
grow faster than either Sylvester or Sasha could prune
them.

The picture Sylvester finally settled on was *F.I.S.T.*
He accepted it because it fit the criteria of being a
prestigious picture with a big-name director and was
different from *Rocky* in one important sense. As
Sylvester described it, "Rocky was a character who
was led by men. In *F.I.S.T.* I play a trucker who is a
leader of men."

*F.I.S.T.* is the epic story of the rise and fall of
Johnny Kovak, head of the powerful Federated Inter-
State Truckers union. The script, by Joe Eszterhas,
had been kicking around Hollywood for several years,
director Norman Jewison *(In the Heat of the Night*
and *Fiddler on the Roof)* having approached such
stars as Al Pacino and Jack Nicholson, trying without
success to interest them in the picture. He'd even gone
to private investors in Germany and Italy to try and
raise money. No one wanted to make *F.I.S.T.* until the
director got in touch with Sylvester. Says Jewison,

"He called me the next day and told me it was one of the best scripts he had ever read and he wanted to do it." Given the fact that Sylvester was so much in demand, a studio was sure to follow.

But Sylvester had some stipulations. As it stood, one of the reasons *F.I.S.T.* had gone unmade was that it would be too long and too expensive to shoot. Sylvester offered to cut it down, to make it more concise. Something else he wanted to do, which he felt was just as important, was to make some changes in the main character. "Johnny Kovak was a dastardly guy," he says, "the most rotten human being to walk the earth. At the end, when he gets killed, we would all cheer. I said I would do the picture if I could tailor the part for me." According to Sylvester, that meant changing him from a heel into a doughtier man "who made deals under duress, but who in the end rectified all of it with intelligent business handling. The labor leader I portray brings dignity to working men."

It should be noted that, once again, Sylvester wasn't insisting on making changes for the sake of throwing around his weight. His philosophy about filmmaking, forged in his ramshackle Hollywood apartment and hardened in the heat of *Rocky*, was simple: "It's necessary for me to play something on screen that is totally accepted. A hero. Otherwise, my art is a device just for a select audience. I'm a great believer in commerciality; it's something that people want to pay for and can understand and recommend to other people. To me, a cult film is something everyone talks about and no one sees." To make certain no one misunderstood and thought he was simply being greedy, he drew an analogy to Picasso, stating that the artist understood how "art and the commercial aspect go hand in hand. That's why he has a $200 million estate whereas other painters are just as good and they bury them in a gunnysack in Potter's field."

Jewison didn't necessarily subscribe to the idea that sophistication and mass appeal represented an either–or situation, but he didn't see anything wrong with Sylvester rewriting the script. After all, the man had written *Rocky*. His only provision was that Sylvester make the changes in his presence, something that would allow him to help shape the material as it was being written. Sylvester knew that it would be an extremely difficult way to write ("Think about it," he says, "it's like *Beat the Clock!*"), but he agreed, the character changes were made—primarily the fleshing out of Johnny's love interest—the script was reduced by more than a third, the alterations brought the proposed budget down to $8 million, and United Artists, hot on their "discovery" of Sylvester, agreed to make the picture. Sylvester's fee for the film was a half-million dollars.

Sylvester went into the film with characteristic dedication. He read everything he could find about the labor movement, becoming an expert on the lives and times of Walter Reuther, John L. Lewis, Samuel Gompers, and Jimmy Hoffa. At the same time, as in *Rocky*, he immediately put himself on a special diet; only this time around it wasn't shrimp but "bananas and water, which wasn't a laugh riot. In fact, it left me bordering on lunacy. But bananas contain potassium, which stimulates the nerve synapses." That, he says, made him more able to play the electric, ever-alert Kovak. Moreover, as Kovak aged, Sylvester stayed in character and also aged. He ate a lot of rich foods to develop a paunch, and, Sylvester laughs, people who saw him actually thought he was going to pot (he says he heard one person mutter, "Look at Stallone—he's turning into a regular warthog!"). He says he "also took to shuffling around at home like an old man, and my wife hated it, the housekeeper hated it, my kid hated it— even Butkus hated it."

Strictly speaking, what he calls hate was really bemusement, the Stallone household wondering if Sylvester had simply lost a wheel. Elsewhere in Hollywood, however, hate was precisely what a number of people were feeling toward Sylvester.

It's a fact of Hollywood that when someone is riding high, whether a star or a director, the innately envious industry wants to see him or her whittled down to size, especially when the person is perceived to have been an overnight success. Nowadays, having "paid his dues" with flops galore and managing to return from the professional dead, Sylvester is accepted and even lauded. But back in July of 1977, when *F.I.S.T.* went before the cameras, he was a big target, and everyone took shots at him.

"The whole experience of the making of *F.I.S.T.* was very unpleasant," he declares, and he states that it "wasn't worth the seven months I spent making it."

To begin with, he went into the picture with a terrible burden on his shoulders. Since he'd started in Hollywood, Sylvester had been managed by Jane Oliver, one of the sweetest and most compassionate people in the business. She'd held Sylvester's hand through the rough spots in his career, counseling him and serving as what he calls "the stabilizing force." Unknown to him, she'd been dying of cancer and hadn't wanted to trouble him with the fact. He learned of it when he called Jane's home one day and was informed by her husband that she had died. The guilt and desolation he felt were unparalleled, and he went into *F.I.S.T.* feeling angry and lost.

Fueling those emotions were a series of problems that cropped up on location. The scenes set in the thirties were shot in Dubuque, Iowa, because, according to production manager Larry DeWaay, it had "good period buildings" and, since the city was extensively serviced by cable, "there weren't any television antennas to worry about."

The most persistent difficulty Sylvester faced was the wrath of the locals. Though he would chat with fans and pose for pictures quite often, it wasn't enough to satisfy everyone. He says that while he was perfectly willing to set aside some time each day, "the security situation during the entire shooting of the film was mediocre. I was bothered *all the time* by fans." This created a lot of tension and, worse, a large percentage of the approximately 500 Iowans who were employed as craftspeople or as extras quickly came to hate him outright. He says, "I know many extras thought I was stuck up, but I'm not. Hell, I was an extra myself not too long ago. But I firmly believe that an actor should remain solitary if he hopes to act with 100 percent efficiency. If I were to go around chatting, much of my energy would be skimmed off. We all have a bank of creativity, but if we use it up in idle talk, then it's wasted and we have nothing to call upon when it's really needed." He went on with exasperation, "I've *always* believed that. When I used to play football, I'd never talk to a soul before a game. I knew it would sap my strength and energy."

In this matter, Jewison came to Sylvester's defense. Says the director, the energy the actor stores allows him to perform "with total abandonment," which Jewison admired. "He's one of the few actors in the business today who isn't introspective. He plays every part with honesty."

But Sylvester had his problems with Jewison as well. "I didn't think I was being treated right," he says. "Norman was staying in a $2500-a-month house and I was in a $70-a-week hotel, a real rat trap. Norman's next to a country club listening to the birds, and I'm in my room listening to the pipes rattle." But Sylvester says he could have lived with that if everything else had been on course. As it was, he admits, "If I were on the set for another day or two there would have been some tremendous volcanic explosions. There was no script communication after the filming started. There was no one to talk to. Nobody asked me what I thought about anything. There was never one day of rehearsal. We just walked onto the set and would wing it."

To top it off, Sylvester was subjected to the anger of *F.I.S.T.*'s screenwriter.

No screenplay ever goes from the scripter's typewriter to the screen as written. Not only do the actors and director bring fresh insight to the story, but new

ideas always crop up during the course of shooting. If
the writer is on the set, he or she is usually offered the
opportunity to make the changes; otherwise, the director and/or the actors do it. Writers tend to resent that,
but, as Sylvester points out, when an actor comes
aboard he or she is "going to tailor something to their
body."

In the case of *F.I.S.T.*, Stallone had requested from
the start that he be credited as coauthor of the screenplay. From his point of view, the request was reasonable. "If there is more than 40 percent of Eszterhas's
original dialogue left in the film," he said, "I would be
very surprised. I worked for five months on total
speculation; I never received a dime, not one penny.
They brought me a script as thick as a telephone book.
It needed pacing, tempo—it was too long, a seven-
hour movie." He didn't ask for the profit participation
usually accorded screenwriters, which had rewarded
him so handsomely on *Rocky,* and he didn't ask to
have a hand in writing the novel based on the screenplay or to share any of the money paid for it (a
towering $400,000, a record sum for a novelization).
He says, "The title *F.I.S.T.* alone is worth the
$400,000!"

Another reason Sylvester wanted credit was so he
could do some image making. People intuitively regarded him as a dumb lug, and he resented it. "I'm
usually taken for a person of limited intelligence," he
confided much later. "I don't know why, but I figure
it's because physically I don't look intelligent, like a
man of letters. I guess people assume the scripts are
delivered to me under the door." Each credit he col-

lected under his belt would, he hoped, help to slowly change that impression. Regarding the matter of *F.I.S.T.*, he summed it up by stating sadly, "All I wanted was partial credit, and Joe resisted."

Actually, "resisted" isn't quite the word. Frustrated beyond words, Eszterhas took his case to the press, where, in Sylvester's words, he said "some slanderous things" about him. Sylvester was referring primarily to an interview that appeared in a Dubuque newspaper wherein Eszterhas was quoted as saying that Stallone wanted to "steal my script [and] muscle in on two years of my research . . . feeding his ego by getting the credit."

The debate raged on, the men trading blows in the press, the situation deteriorating even further when Sylvester and Eszterhas were charged with plagiarism. Says Sylvester of that imbroglio, "All I did was rewrite what I thought was an original screenplay . . . and now this guy I've never heard of, Lionel White, is supposedly suing us for plagiarism. I never stole a line from anyone in my life!"

Regardless of which side the filmmakers were on, everyone agreed that the making of *F.I.S.T.* was a nightmare. However, unlike most nightmares, this was one destined not to end.

# Chapter

## Eight

The biggest dispute about *F.I.S.T.* occurred when
shooting was over, and it involved how to end the film.
*F.I.S.T.* had been shot with three different endings:
one in which Kovak disappears, Hoffa-like; one in
which, in Sylvester's words, "I'm shot to pieces"; and
another in which he is censured by a Senate committee, after which, as Sylvester describes it, "he looks
toward the Senate building and throws up his fist in
defiance because he knows he still has the power to
shut the country down by keeping every truck off the
road."

Shooting multiple endings is not uncommon in mov-
iemaking. Sometimes it's necessary for the filmmakers
to watch a film up until the climax before deciding

which way the story should go; at other times they let
the public decide, showing one ending to one audience
and a different ending to another audience. Whichever
one gets the most favorable reaction is the one they
use.

In the matter of *F.I.S.T.*, however, there was a
complicating factor: Sylvester's concept of heroism
and morality. Thus, how to end the picture became the
next big, very public battleground.

Sylvester says that while he was rewriting *F.I.S.T.*
he had had dreams of making it "a landmark film, the
ultimate blue-collar movie." To this end, he felt
strongly that at the picture's climax Kovak should
throw up his fist. "It's a definite upper," he told New
York's *Daily News*, "just as the *Rocky* finish was. To
have Kovak die is a total downer. For him to die is for
the American labor movement to die; my ending has a
lot to do with the American way of life, which is
always to bounce back after defeat."

Jewison didn't. agree, but, to be on the safe side, he
tested two of the endings with audiences, Sylvester's
and—his own preference—the disappearance. He reports, "There was no difference in the audience reaction" and, describing Sylvester's ending as "unsatisfactory," said that in order to be true to himself he had
to go with what he felt was the most realistic, most
appropriate ending. Sylvester was livid.

"I *wish* I had some say," he complained at the time,
"but I don't. I must have told him my views over fifty
times, but it [didn't] do any good." Indeed, so well
known was Sylvester's displeasure that when Jewison
appeared in public with his arm in a cast, the director

was moved to note, "It's not true that Sylvester
Stallone broke my arm over the ending." He grinned,
then added, "United Artists did."

According to Sylvester, Jewison's decision spelled
disaster for the picture. He cited as precedent the
diminished returns for *Chinatown*. That 1974 film
ended with Faye Dunaway being shot to death by John
Huston while a stunned Jack Nicholson looks on.
"That was the worst ending I ever saw," Sylvester
claims. "Everyone who saw that movie was hoping
that somehow Dunaway would be able to salvage
something from her miserable life by going away with
Nicholson, the man she loved. I couldn't believe the
ending." And what made it worse, he insisted, was
that there was no reason for it. "They were in a
position of making it upbeat without damaging the
picture at all."

Nor did Sylvester stop after decrying the aesthetics
of the decision. He believed that filmmakers who
resorted to downers were lazy. "It's very simple to
write a downer," he said. "You just write, 'The guy
falls into the subway train's path and is ground into
chicken fat.' But to say he falls onto the track and at
the last second leaps beneath the train or somehow
slithers between the rails . . . that's tougher to write,
but to me it's more enjoyable."

In addition to offending Sylvester's idealism, Jewison upset his star even more when he edited the
picture in what Sylvester felt was an inept, emascu-
lated fashion.

When a movie is made, scenes are frequently filmed
several times with the actor giving cold or hot read-

ings—that is, playing it low-keyed or really letting go. This gives the director some creative leeway when assembling the finished film.

In the case of *F.I.S.T.*, Sylvester says, "I don't know why, but Norman Jewison never used my most fiery takes, so I came off lukewarm throughout the movie." According to Sylvester, that made the picture seem plodding. What's more, he says that several critical scenes were left out of the finished film.

"I started off in *F.I.S.T.* talking the way I'm talking now," he says, "and then my voice got lower and I finally ended up talking in a hoarse whisper. But the transition scenes weren't used, so you wonder where Johnny Kovak's voice came from. That really burned me up because it looked like I didn't do my homework, and I *did*."

But "the biggest blow," according to Sylvester, concerned a line that was deleted from the scene when Johnny is grilled at a Senate hearing. He says he never worked harder juicing himself up for a scene and ended up with "heart palpitations, blurred vision—I actually thought I was gonna go into a nervous breakdown. Anyway," he continues, "at the end of my confrontation with Rod Steiger, I get up and say, 'I hold you in contempt, I hold this hearing in contempt, and most of all I hold *myself* in contempt!' I then walk to the hearing-room door and I turn around and shout, 'You may bring *me* down, but you're not gonna bring this union down—or we're gonna shut this *country* down.'" Sylvester's intention was to make this Kovak's last roar, the "bellowing of a dying bull." But Jewison felt that it was too menacing, and cut the scene before Johnny delivered the coup de grace. That was bad enough, says Sylvester, but what bothered him more was that "I'd paced my performance for that moment, which is why I didn't go all the way when confronting Steiger. I wanted to save that last little bit extra for that line—which would've put a different edge on the scene and on the picture."

But Sylvester had no authority in the matter of editing *F.I.S.T.,* and his pleas went unheeded. He describes the frustration he felt on finally seeing the finished film: it was "like giving the blueprints of a house to a construction team and not going back until it's built—and then you wind up saying, 'My God, they've put the kitchen in the bedroom and the bedroom in the basement, and everything's wrong!' Most of my efforts were butchered."

Because of his disappointment with the film, Sylvester refused to do any publicity for it. His feeling was that since it was Jewison's film, Jewison should promote it—though he knew full well that the public couldn't care less about the director of a film.

Whether or not Sylvester's suggestions would have made a difference will never be known. As it turned out, when *F.I.S.T.* opened in April of 1978, it was a major commercial disappointment. Not that it was a bad movie; it was, however, too lower-class for the audience that had turned out for *The Godfather, Part II*—to which it was frequently and unfavorably compared—and it was too plodding and downbeat for the people who had found *Rocky* so endearing. The picture made back its cost, returning $9.5 million to United Artists. That wasn't bad, but it was hardly

what the studio had expected from Sylvester's first
film after *Rocky*.

Ironically, in the interest of clearing the air before
the picture opened, Sylvester and Eszterhas had actually made up at the opening, the actor going so far as to
take full blame for everything that had happened. If
he'd hoped the gods were listening and would smile on
them, he was wrong.

By the fall of 1977, though the film had yet to open,
the various *F.I.S.T.* fights had earned Sylvester a
reputation as one of the biggest egomaniacs in the film
industry. Columnist Rex Reed seemed to be speaking
for many people when he wrote in the *Daily News,*
"Instead of a head, Sylvester Stallone carries on his
shoulder an ego the size of a forty-pound eggplant."
Everyone seemed to be badmouthing him, even old
friends and colleagues who couldn't understand why
he wasn't looking out for them now that he'd succeeded. (Their attitude was the inspiration for what
Paulie would become in the first two *Rocky* sequels, a
bitter, hateful man who felt forgotten by the champ.)

It was a lambasting Sylvester hardly deserved, and
virtually the only people in Hollywood who went out
of their way to defend "the wandering dramaturge" (a
term he playfully said he prefers to "star") were Rod
Steiger, who played a Senator in *F.I.S.T.,* and Carl
Weathers.

"I was wondering how he took success," Steiger
said, "that being the true barometer of the man, and he
seems to have taken it well. I found him very nice and
very respectful." But, Steiger concedes, between the

pressure from peers and fans, "the poor guy never got a moment's peace [and] I began to feel sorry for him." Weathers agreed, telling one reporter, "Listen, I'm very egocentric myself. The thing is, you have to control egos, and I think he has his under control."

But they were voices shouting in the wilderness, and, partly because of advance word on the limpness of *F.I.S.T.* and partly because of the desire to see Sylvester fail, cries of "one-hit star" and "washed up" could be heard all over Hollywood. That bothered Sylvester a great deal, not just because of his ego but because he was afraid it would become a self-fulfilling prophecy. Some of that concern had begun to surface during the shooting of *F.I.S.T.* in Dubuque, when Sylvester had cohosted "The Mike Douglas Show." At one point, Douglas turned to Sylvester and said, "It'll be interesting to see if they're calling you Rocky or Johnny or Sly after this picture." Nodding, Sylvester replied in earnest, "I don't care . . . just so they call me." He admits that the more gossip he heard about his fading star, the more he "discovered real fear for the first time, fear of losing what I had attained. Before, I didn't care. I was broke."

He didn't know how to change people's opinions of him, since he'd never faced anything even remotely like this. No one believed him when he told the press, "I really don't walk around thinking, 'I am *so* celestial. I am not of this earth. I twinkle in the cosmos while all of you grovel in the valleys.'" And not knowing what to do made things worse, since he says he became "brusque with people . . . hard . . . because people are coming at me with undue malevolence."

But he did know that professionally he would do what he could to protect himself, which meant never again "putting my fate in someone else's hands" if it could be helped. To that end, even though *F.I.S.T.* was months away from opening, he settled in at Universal to get *Paradise Alley* under way *his* way—as writer, star, and director. Naturally, when the industry heard that Sylvester was now going to be directing as well as writing and starring, the voices of doom grew louder still.

Fortunately, their cries as well as the concerns Sylvester had about his flagging popularity were softened somewhat by the forty-sixth annual poll of motion picture exhibitors, which named him the top box-office draw in the country, placing him ahead of such megastars as Robert Redford and Clint Eastwood. Universal was also glad to hear it and, turning a deaf ear to what the rest of Hollywood was saying, paved the way for *Paradise Alley* by having their Putnam books division publish Sylvester's novel.

Unfortunately, instead of the huge bestseller they were expecting, Universal ended up with a critical and commercial disaster on their hands. Reviewers slammed the work's "too, too solid prose" (*Newsweek*), and Sylvester himself was trashed for having "no verbal imagination whatever" *(The New York Times)*. If he'd been unhappy and scared before, he was positively miserable now.

But Sylvester tried to put the catastrophic reviews from his mind as he plunged into *Paradise Alley,* approaching the job of directing as he did any new experience, with typical confidence and optimism. He

said, "Directing is like playing chess with people. I'm
learning how the other half lives."

*Paradise Alley* had been changed only slightly from
its original story. It was still a tale of the three Carboni
brothers searching for a magic carpet ride out of Hell's
Kitchen in 1946; only now they planned to earn their
fame and fortune using the talents of brother Victor
(Lee Canalito) as wrestler "Kid Salami." Sylvester
starred as the hustling middle brother Cosmo, with
Armand Assante as their older, embittered sibling
Lenny. Love interest for Sylvester was provided by
Joyce Ingalls.

As before, Sylvester got ready for the movie by
putting himself on a customized diet. "I got into
energy foods," he says. "Nuts, fruits, juices, and
things that go through your system very easily, like
pulverized chicken. I ate like that because I wanted to
devote all my energy to directing, writing, and acting."

Geared up for the challenge of directing and proving
the doomsayers wrong, Sylvester went back to New
York in January of 1978 to shoot the *Paradise Alley*
exteriors. Actually, the picture was shot primarily on
West 80th Street, a tad north of Hell's Kitchen, because little had changed there since the forties. All the
set designers had to do was bring over 1946-style
lampposts, trashcans, automobiles, and window dress-
ing. Other locations included docks along the Hudson
River and the Knickerbocker Icehouse in Brooklyn.

Despite Sylvester's experiences in Dubuque and his
unpleasant memories of the Big Apple ("I died in New
York and was reborn in Hollywood, and I owe my
allegience to that town"), he was relatively outgoing

with the New York fans, in part because they were so proud of the neighborhood boy who'd made good and also because he was constantly being watched by a man-mountain named Tony, his new personal bodyguard. Even so, one night a large woman did manage to slip past a restraining rope and, making her way to the star, jump on his back. To his credit, the nervous Sylvester did not deck her nor did he banish fans from the location. He did, however, order all press off the set one afternoon when Earl Wilson published a column criticizing his attitude toward photographers. He'd simply had enough of being criticized and reasoned that if he were going to get grilled anyway, why waste his time giving interviews or being sociable?

Removing the newspeople, however, didn't spare Sylvester entirely from criticism. Standing on the sidelines, one woman noted, "He looked so much bigger on the screen. He's a little squirt!" However, another fan was there to defend his honor, shouting back, "Who cares? That's Rocky on 80th Street, honey!"

Among the first bits of "information" the press published about *Paradise Alley* was that Sylvester was steadfastly refusing to hire any actor who was taller than he. That claim was refuted easily enough when Sylvester pointed out to one sympathetic journalist that "there're at least nine actors who are not only bigger than me, they're half the size of the island of Rhodes."

However, the second rumor to emerge from the set turned out to be the truth, that Sylvester was having an affair, and it drove the biggest wedge yet into the Stallones' already shaky marriage.

The third party was Joyce Ingalls, and Sasha says, "I don't think Sly expected to become as involved with her as he did." According to Sylvester's wife, Sylvester and Joyce became involved solely because they were working together, which is common enough in Hollywood. On a movie, actors are involved intimately, emotionally, and for so many hours day after day that they become surrogate family to one another. If there's a sexual attraction, they often become lovers.

At first, Sylvester was too busy to have an affair. Sasha came to visit him in New York and notes that he was preoccupied with the logistics of getting everything shot on time and within the budget. Then she left and, concurrently, he admits "the pressures got to me." He handled it by "playing hooky from reality" with Joyce and "directing my frustrations at the people I love most, simply because they were the most vulnerable to attack."

When Sasha found out about Joyce from anti-Stallone factions on the set, she went through a rapid succession of emotions. At first, she says, "I was frightened and distraught. Then I was furious. We had been on the bottom *together,* and when he made it to the top he wanted to go it *alone.*"

As it happened, Sylvester didn't know what he wanted. "I flipped out," he says. "I was moving on a fast track, and when you're going that fast, it's hard to keep the scenery in view—it becomes a blur."

Rather than go along for the ride, Sasha filed for divorce in March, though it wasn't a run-of-the-mill separation. Sylvester came home three or four days each week, at which time the couple tried to see if the damage was irreversible. It was not. "Our sex life was still passionate," Sasha reveals, "and he was still very attached to the baby. He remained very involved as a father and husband." Just as important, since they now saw each other less, they had more to talk about when they were together. That helped to break up the communication bottleneck. Sylvester also became less critical of Sasha, a problem she says had surfaced when he became so profoundly dissatisfied with his own state of affairs.

What the separation also accomplished was to help Sasha realize that "there was a part of me that wanted freedom too," and she used the time that was now entirely hers to get her photographic career on track. She signed with an agent and began accepting assignments. She also became a fitness buff, did more scuba diving, and became involved in the women's movement.

About the only thing she didn't do was see other men. Joyce Ingalls notwithstanding, Sasha says that Sylvester "came right out and said that he didn't want me to date anyone else." She adds that if she had gone out with anyone, "Sly . . . would have punched [him] in the nose." But she didn't really want to be with anyone but herself and her son, and she adds with a smile that, in any case, "Sly would be a hard act to follow."

After a while, it became apparent that the separation was the only thing that managed to work out right for Sylvester. It lasted four months. Sasha told *The Ladies' Home Journal* that it ended one night when

Sylvester "called and said he wanted to come over to discuss our future. He came over and said he needed his roots; the baby and I were his foundation. He wanted to come home to stay." Sylvester himself adds that the reconciliation would have happened sooner, since he "wanted to go home badly." But he "waited and waited for the proper opportunity—until I realized there is no such thing. You just have to strip yourself down to the bare wires and do it."

Sasha was glad to take him back, though she did stipulate that she wasn't about to go back to their "old patterns." She told him that she intended to continue with her various outside activities, and Sylvester agreed, the couple rather dramatically making the announcement at the world premiere of *F.I.S.T.*—the same occasion where the repentant Sylvester also mended the fence with Joe Eszterhas. Sylvester apologized to Sasha for "having destroyed the tranquility of my family and publicly embarrassing my wife and friends"; as he later put it, that was a night for "swallowing a lot of crow."

But it was a fortuitous move on Sylvester's part, not only because the relationship had been salvaged but also because he was about to need all the support he could get. In addition to *F.I.S.T.* opening and dying, *Paradise Alley* suffered the same fate when it opened in November. In fact, it was an even worse debacle on two fronts: it made less money than *F.I.S.T.* by nearly half (it finally crept into the black with revenues from TV sales), and there was no passing the buck for this failure. *Paradise Alley* sat squarely on Sylvester's shoulders.

Then and there, the saga of Sylvester Stallone might have come to a sad, decidedly un-*Rocky*-esque end. Luckily, before the disastrous opening of *Paradise Alley,* Sylvester had come to terms with United Artists on another film. Once again he would write, star, and direct. But this time it was a picture that would kick him from the cellar back to box-office dominance.

# Chapter

## Nine

"There is this one question which when I hear it makes me very mad. They all ask me, 'Will *Rocky II* save your career?' Is this my comeback? they wanna know. Will it pull my career out of the toilet?" Sylvester shook his head. "I've never made a film that lost money, but after *Rocky* was such an enormous success *anything* was gonna be an anticlimax."

While Sylvester minimizes the degree to which *F.I.S.T.* and *Paradise Alley* had failed, he was correct in pointing out that reports of his professional death had been greatly exaggerated. There were still plenty of scripts for him to read. He did *Rocky II* largely because, after all he'd been through, he needed a "resuscitator" to help him "regain the same sensibilities I had when I was writing *Rocky*."

Still, he knew that *Rocky II* was a critical picture for him. If it did only as well as most movie sequels— approximately 60 percent of the original box office— then it would prove nothing about his abilities as a filmmaker. Even a bad sequel can usually hit that magic number. Sylvester wanted to make the most successful sequel in film history and was determined to make a movie that, technically and artistically, would knock the first one back on its heels.

Needless to say, critics who said that Sylvester was simply returning to the well not only annoyed him but also hadn't checked the record. Sylvester had been talking about sequels to the film even before *Rocky* opened.

"If you have a character that's well liked," he's said, "and if you can use the character in a successful film that has a message applicable to today, why desert him? Killing them off is just too Hemingwayesque for me." Besides, he went on, "As a writer, I've always been interested in the trilogy form, like the *Studs Lonigan* trilogy of James Farrell. It would be pretty tough to tell the whole story of a man's life in an hour and forty-five minutes." He scowled. "But that word *sequel* automatically means trash to a lot of people, and I don't know why. I mean, a novelist writes a story, breaks it up into three books, and he calls it a trilogy. People don't say, 'What is this trilogy crap?' They accept that an artist has a three-part story. But you make several movies that are one story and the world dumps on you. Well, I'm telling the world I don't care."

He did, however, fluctuate frequently about where

he wanted the character of Rocky to go. On the one hand, part of him wanted to have Rocky wrest the title from Apollo in the second film and in *Rocky III* have a final fight in the Roman Colosseum. Yet Sylvester also wondered openly if he shouldn't go in another direction entirely, having Rocky attend night school and then enter politics, either going to Washington—thus making the Capra connection complete—or running for mayor of Philadelphia as in his pre-*Rocky* tale of the righteous cab driver. With the political angle, Sylvester reasoned that the third film of the series could have Rocky run afoul of the political machine because he was "too honest," find himself impeached, and end up back in the ring as a contented and upright has-been.

Ultimately, he elected to stick solely to the boxing motif for two amazingly disparate reasons. Before sitting down to write the script for *Rocky II,* he happened to be going through a renewed phase of reading Puritan literature. He was struck that the theme recurring throughout was "the duel between the flesh and the spirit." That had been the core of the first Rocky film, and he decided that if something 300 years old still made good reading, who was he to discard it for a movie sequel?

Then too, from a purely commercial rather than aesthetic standpoint, the boxing ring provided something for audiences that was in dramatically short supply: virility.

"I don't think that even women's lib wants all men to become limp-wristed librarians," he said with a wink, then continued more seriously, "but I don't know what is happening to men these days. There's a trend toward a sleek, subdued sophistication. In discos, men and women look almost alike, and if you were a little bleary-eyed you'd get them mixed up. I think it's wrong, and I think women are unhappy about it." *Rocky* had made macho somewhat respectable, and Sylvester earnestly hoped that a second picture set in and around the ring would make it more respectable still.

Before *Paradise Alley,* Sylvester had said that if he continued the saga of Rocky he wanted Avildsen to direct. However, he decided to helm this one himself for several reasons. For one thing, *Paradise Alley* was hardly a sterling directorial debut, even though he was proud of how "free-formish" it was in terms of visual technique. He wanted to establish himself as a director more securely with *Rocky II.* For another, there were a number of things he wanted to do differently from *Rocky,* and, clearly, he didn't want these changes to be a matter of debate.

"A common mistake," he said, voicing his biggest complaint about the first film, "is that the cameramen were framing too close. In a fight film, you can't frame any frame any tighter than from the bottom of the boxer's shorts to the top of his head—otewise it becomes a blur of bodies. Also, the majority of the fight was shot through the ropes, which has a tendency to block out a lot of the action." He didn't blame Avildsen for any of this, acknowledging that many decisions were dictated by a lack of time and budget. Still, with so much riding on the film, he had to be in control. As he put it, "The only thing that could cause

*Rocky II* to miss would be a thing called magic," and he was going to work like a demon to achieve it.

Not that he strayed from the style established by Avildsen. The moviegoing public wouldn't have stood for it. Sylvester says, "John was pretty straight-ahead, so *Rocky II* I did very literally." He says he "didn't do any of the stuff" he liked in the films of others, such as "being so tight on people in close-ups that the veins in their eyes look like the Mississippi River," or things he had done in *Paradise Alley,* the kinds of quick cuts and montages that "keep people from getting bored" and cause them to think, " 'What's that?' and by the time they see it, it's gone. A little legerdemain." The picture was more like Joe Frazier than Muhammad Ali; more a piledriver than a fancy dancer.

Whether from fear or creative passion, Sylvester poured his heart into the film when shooting commenced in October of 1978, work for which he was both rewarded and punished.

The punishment was primarily physical. When it was over, Sylvester said, "I'm real messed up inside; I took a terrible beating. I let Carl Weathers really pound me, and it was the most grueling thing I've ever been through: broken bones, a bruised kidney, the works. The fight's four times as long, has eight times as many punches as the first one, and a lot of those shots aren't fake." He adds, "Your body has a tendency to go to hell. I was twenty-nine when I was Rocky; now I'm thirty-two. Time doesn't wait."

He admits to having been particularly foolhardy in one off-camera stunt. He told sportswriter Red Smith, "I was working with Franco Columbu, a former Mr.

Olympics I think he's called. Anyway, at the end of the workout he said, 'Let's see you bench press 200 pounds.' I said, 'I'm kind of tired,' but he said, 'Just once.' So I laid back and pressed 200. 'Try 210,' he said, so I did. 'Now 220,' so I tried 220 pounds . . . and I heard a pop. The pain was something awful and pretty soon the arm turned black. I had to go to the doctor." Sylvester remarks that the doctor was so impressed by the injury that he quickly took a picture, explaining that he was writing a medical book and had been looking for a chance to snap just such a photo. Very few people, he explained, were reckless enough to do what Sylvester had done. As a result of the accident, Sylvester says, "I had no lateral movement in the arm. I could punch straight up, a short uppercut, but I couldn't swing a round punch. Fortunately, the script called for me to switch to southpaw then, or we'd have had to cancel the picture."

That doesn't mean he had an easy time of it; Sylvester had opted to shoot the fight first, so he'd have plenty of time to look at the footage and edit it together as dramatically as possible. Thus, he had to shoot the rest of the film still smarting from the ripped pectoralis major and the rest of his injuries. The torn muscle would subsequently require a hospital stay. Says Sylvester, "The whole right side of my chest was torn off; I have a scar that goes all the way down my side like a zipper. They had to drill holes in my sternum and my shoulder blade to tie the muscles back. It was a four-hour operation and I had 156 stitches." He also notes, shuddering, that it was only the seventh successful operation of its kind.

Originally, when he'd talked about making more Rocky films, Sylvester had wanted to keep their budgets within the $3 million range so they'd have the same tight, gritty flavor of the original. But when he went back and studied *Rocky,* he decided against that approach. Back then, he said, "since we didn't have a crowd of spectators, 85 to 90 percent of the fight was shot from low angles," which he knew would be boring in the new film. He wanted to be able to "drop back and really see the canvas and the action." He also wanted to be able to have more cameras covering the fight—six in addition to slow-motion cameras. And, of course, he had to pay his Rocky family more for their services. Therefore, he ended up with a budget eight times that of the original and a movie that took an astonishing eight months to make. Less than two months of that was actual shooting time; the rest was spent in the editing room, where Sylvester concentrated on making the fight brutally realistic, one which through "the slow motion and sound effects" would communicate to audiences "exactly what it's like to get hit." So singlemindedly did Sylvester work on the fight that producer Winkler finally had to get "two guys to pick me up and carry me out of the editing room."

*Rocky II* opened in June of 1979, and in many respects it managed to fulfill Sylvester's ambition to make a superior film. Technically, the sequel is infinitely better than the first. More important, however, the character grows a great deal. He marries and gives up boxing at Adrian's urging. Meanwhile, having bettered himself materially, he finds that he's in over his head and has to accept the humiliation of doing menial labor and seeing his pregnant wife take a job. Just as significantly, Rocky also has to deal with an "Italian Chicken" campaign launched by Apollo to coax him back into the ring. This time around Rocky even cries, weeping by the side of his wife as she lies comatose after giving birth to Rocky Jr. Sylvester says he discovered that crying was (and still is) one of the most difficult things for him to do as an actor, not because of any kind of misplaced machoism but from a purely technical standpoint. "Sometimes when I don't want to cry, I cry. And when I want to, I can't. It's interesting how perverse the subconscious is; I wish I could master that." He likens it to sex, stating, "When you think, 'Ah, tonight's the night,' well . . . But then when you think, 'Just let me get home and get right to sleep,' it winds up you're swinging from the rafters."

The script is also filled with little gems which result from Sylvester himself having lived more, having experienced the ups and downs of fame. In addition to the sycophantic Paulie, there are opportunists who try to make a buck off Rocky by casting him in TV commercials and businesspeople who regard Rocky as too "narrow" and refuse to hire him for a desk job he knows he can do (Sylvester's acting range was similarly criticized). Then there are the fans who bother the hero for autographs even when he's lying in a hospital bed, barely able to write. The first film was Sylvester with his nose pressed to the window of fame and success; the second picture is the insider's report. And while there's a sense of déjà vu in the robust training routine (complete with the stirring Bill Conti music), the endless bickering with Mickey, and the blustering of Apollo Creed, there was no way around the fact that these are, after all, the same characters, and the picture does begin just minutes after the climactic bout in the first film. But the picture is brimming with Sylvester's love for the characters, and, considering that Sylvester no longer had the novelty value of the little-guy-triumphing theme to work with, he did a superlative job.

*Rocky II* also shows Sylvester's affection for his audience, which was greater than ever. In addition to the millions who had seen the picture in theaters, *Rocky* had recently aired on TV and boasted the third largest audience that had ever watched a movie on television (trailing only *Gone with the Wind* and *Airport 1975*).

"Including television," Sylvester said, "about 265 million people saw *Rocky*. This one had to be just as good, and the whole team agreed that we'd walk away before we would grind out a potboiler to capitalize on Rocky." To his credit, Sylvester felt so strongly about both the characters and his fans that he turned down an incredible $3 million offer to put on boxing gloves and box for three rounds with Muhammad Ali. While it would have been a tremendous publicity stunt, Sylvester says, "Sure, I could go around in boxing gloves and do exhibitions all the time and make millions and millions of dollars. But it's not worth it. Can you imagine what people would think, to exploit Rocky in that way?"

Sylvester's high regard for his public paid off with *Rocky II* going through the roof. It earned 90 percent as much money as the original, a historic showing that made it the most successful movie sequel in history and brought Sylvester's haul from the two *Rocky* pictures to $25 million. About the only satisfaction he was denied was critical acceptance. There were no Oscar nominations this time around, and the reviews were tepid at best. That bothered Sylvester a great deal since, if nothing else, he knew that his own performance was better and more assured. Since Al Pacino had been nominated for Oscars for both *Godfather* films, Sylvester couldn't understand how he could be slighted after giving a stronger performance. But he comforted himself with the fact that the public not only queued up for the picture but also purchased millions of *Rocky II* tie-ins, from souvenir magazines to bubble gum cards. The critics may have turned their backs on him, but the public still loved their Italian Stallion. And they were not alone.

Shortly after they'd gotten back together, Sasha had become pregnant with their second child. In May, Seargeoh (pronounced "Sergio" and nicknamed Seth) was born. All seemed well at the time. Sylvester even joked with the press about the naming of his son. "We wanted all S's in our family," he said. "It's amazing what you do when you don't have a hobby." On a somewhat more serious note, he also explained that the reason he would never name a son Sylvester Jr. was because any boy of his would have a difficult enough time going through life with "kids calling them 'Rocky's kids' and saying things like, 'Your daddy's not so tough.' To meet that challenge," he concluded, "they'll have to know they're individuals."

Then, a mere two months after this portrait of supreme domesticity, Sylvester dropped a bombshell by moving out of the house to live with his new girlfriend, supermodel Susan Anton.

The romance had come on very suddenly, to say the least. Sylvester had bumped into the twenty-nine-year-old Anton at the trendy Studio 54 in New York, having come to town to promote *Rocky II*. She was stumping for her first feature, *Goldengirl,* appropriately enough the story of an athlete. The radiant Southern California girl had been married for four years to Jack Stein, her manager, and insists, "Neither Sly nor I were looking to meet other people, to end our marriages. But it just happened."

Anton says that she and Sylvester chatted briefly at the disco, and then "the next day, by some quirk of fate, we were on the same plane for Los Angeles. There was an instant communication, one of those intangible *clicks*," and she knew there was no turning back. The two started seeing each other, and Anton says, "each time we met the attraction was stronger. Finally, we realized we loved each other."

Actually, it wasn't quite as simple as that, since there are telling parallels between the Ingalls and Anton affairs. Directing a picture is something that has always proven unhealthy for Sylvester's home life. He says, "You go for the glory and you don't think about the repercussions. You don't realize that work is gonna take 99 percent of your time and that to make up for it the 1 percent when you're at home has to be incredibly blissful, tranquil, and sincere." And that, of course, was "just not easy to do because I take home the characters I play."

Directing *Rocky II* made the Stallones' home life tense all over again, and while he didn't want to leave, the success of the picture was the last straw. As he puts it in his characteristically colorful fashion, "I got stroked so much I felt like a 185-pound blister." He was a red-hot property again and says that once more he had "360-degree vision. I saw everything around me, and the last place I wanted to be was at home stifled with the responsibility of a wife and two kids." Anton was his ticket out.

The couple set up housekeeping in Malibu, in a house nestled on three and a half choice beachfront acres (Susan smarmily referred to it as their "little slice of heaven"). Sasha filed for divorce all over again, and the lovebirds said they would marry as soon as their mutual divorces were final. "Sly is very moral; he wouldn't have it any other way," Anton gushed. "And eventually I want to have a child with him; family is very important to both of us."

That may have been true, but, as fate would have it, their own little family didn't last long. The relationship ended just nine months after it had begun. Sylvester went to New York to make a film called *Attack* (which was later changed to *Hawks* and finally *Nighthawks*), and Anton remained behind. The factor most often cited for the breakup is that the stars' demanding schedules left them no time to nurture a private life, and, unlike Sasha, Susan didn't want to give up her career to be a housewife.

Then too, this second affair had shown Sylvester that Sasha's loyalty was more valuable than anything another woman could offer. "Let me put it on a real crass level," he said. "Love is like a new car. The

leather smells great for a while, and it's so exciting to
drive it around and show it off to your people. You
keep it shined and polished. You make love to it, you
might say. Eventually it gets old. But you know what?
As long as it keeps running and is reliable, you keep it
around. You change the tires, keep it tuned up, and it's
reliable. Okay," he concluded, "*that's* love." That's
what he'd had with Sasha, and he wanted it back.

Once again it took him a while to gather his courage
and ask for her forgiveness. Shortly after finishing
*Nighthawks*, Sylvester sold the house in Malibu and
went to Hungary to make a film entitled *Victory*.
Lonely and nostalgic, he finally called Sasha, who
canceled plans to fly to Hawaii for her birthday and
came over. There, on the banks of the Danube,
Sylvester wooed her with such self-censuring lines as
"You're looking at a fully grown fool" and "You have
every reason in the world to despise me." Sylvester
says proudly that she took him back despite what he'd
done to her a second time, "which shows," he says
"that our marriage was right in the first place."

Once again, all would be right with the world.
Unfortunately, as was becoming a habit with Sylvester, both his personal and professional bliss would be
short-lived.

John Rambo prepares to hold off the National Guard in *First Blood*. NBC PHOTO.

Sylvester's high school
yearbook photo. AP PHOTO.

Sylvester Stallone in a publicity photograph from *Rocky*. AP
PHOTO.

Sylvester stays in shape by working out at home and at a local gym. AP PHOTO.

Sylvester and Butkus in the streets of Philadelphia's Kensington section during the shooting of *Rocky*. AP PHOTO.

Sylvester in the driveway of his Malibu home, September 1979. RON GALELLA, LTD.

Sylvester and Sasha. QUINTINO/AP PHOTO.

Sylvester and Brigitte strolling outside New York's Regency
Hotel. AP PHOTO.

Sylvester as Rambo in *Rambo: First Blood Part II*. AP
PHOTO.

# Chapter

## Ten

When he accepted *Nighthawks*, Sylvester still had numerous scripts of his own he wanted to film, among them the Poe story and a rather unusual opus called *Sinsilver*, the story of a Hassidic Jew in the wild west. However, the sting of *Paradise Alley* was still fresh, so he looked elsewhere for material, spending a lot of time after *Rocky II* sifting through the thick stacks of novels publishers and writers had sent him for possible adaptation and scripts that agents and producers wanted him to consider.

Ultimately, Sylvester decided to do *Nighthawks* because it was a bold change-of-pace character for him. *Nighthawks* is the story of a gritty, streetwise decoy cop who is assigned to a crack squadron known

as A.T.A.C. (Anti-Terrorist Action Command) in order
to track a ruthless German terrorist through New
York. Unlike Rocky, Johnny Kovak, or Cosmo Carboni, Sylvester's Sgt. Deke DaSilva is college-edu-
cated and articulate, which gave the actor his first
chance to enunciate in crisp, lean dialogue. It also
allowed him the opportunity to radically change his
look, shedding 35 of his brawny *Rocky II* pounds,
deciding to play the part with eyeglasses, and growing
a lush beard and moustache. So striking was his thin-
ner, hirsute appearance that when filming began the
crew nicknamed him "Baby Jesus." Though the simul-
taneous swipe at his alleged ego was not lost on
Sylvester, he took the teasing good-naturedly.

Signing on to costar with Sylvester were Billy Dee
Williams as DaSilva's tough sidekick Matthew Fox,
and Holland's Rutger Hauer as the terrorist Wulfgar.
Having made a name for himself in the acclaimed
*Soldier of Orange*, Hauer may well have had the
easiest audition of any actor in history. He flew to Los
Angeles for an interview, and so striking were his icy
features that producer Martin Poll recalls, "The min-
ute we met him, Sly and I looked at each other and
nodded." Rounding out the cast were TV's "Bionic
Woman," Lindsay Wagner, as Sylvester's ex-wife
Irene whom he is trying to win back, and India's Persis
Khambatta who, having made a name for herself as a
nymphomaniac, bald-headed alien in *Star Trek: The
Motion Picture*, was signed to play Wulfgar's ruthless
accomplice Shakka.

Before shooting, Sylvester threw himself into researching the part. His special diet this time was

hotdogs and Big Macs as he and Billy Dee Williams spent several weeks traveling around with real decoy cops. If the actor thought he'd seen the worst New York had to offer when he lived there, he was in for a surprise.

After signing releases with the police department and the city stating that they wouldn't sue if they were hurt or killed, Sylvester and Williams were assigned to the Street Crime Unit on Randall's Island for two weeks, tailing the decoys in backup vehicles—one night a cab, the next night an old car, the following night a van. The decoys would dress as businesspeople, students, old women (like Sylvester in the film's opening moments), and the like, and would let themselves get mugged. As soon as that happened, the backup officers would jump out and make the arrest. Williams was surprised to find that "those cops use more makeup than actors," and both actors genuinely admired the courage of these men and women. Sylvester went so far as to get friendly with several of them and was deeply upset shortly after filming began when he learned that one of the decoys he'd gone out with—a man who had already had his throat cut in Sylvester's presence—had been shot and killed.

Sylvester survived his two weeks with the cops, but as soon as shooting got under way he was once again in hot water. Neither of the two controversies was his fault, but that didn't matter. This was a Stallone film, so Stallone was the fall guy.

The first problem occurred shortly after the crew went to New York. Director Gary Nelson was fired by producer Martin Poll, and Bruce Malmuth was hired to take his place. Replacing directors isn't uncommon in Hollywood, and it wouldn't have attracted much press except that Sylvester took over for the day that Malmuth was in transit from Los Angeles.

The Directors Guild has a history of being extremely intractable with film companies that break the rules, and Poll's production was no exception. The rules state that someone can fill in briefly while a director is en route, but only if the location is remote or inaccessible because of weather, a strike, or the like. Midtown Manhattan was not deemed sufficiently off the beaten track, and the Guild ruled that either Malmuth could have taken an earlier flight or the filmmakers could have waited until he arrived.

Despite the fact that the scene Sylvester had shot was little more than an action scene in which DaSilva chases Wulfgar through a subway, the production was fined a substantial $50,000. The filmmakers were angry, but the fact of the matter was that they came out ahead. If they'd shut down for the day, it would have cost them nearly double that in wages. However, according to the *Daily News,* adding insult to injury was the fact that the Guild and Universal both sent representatives to the set to make sure that Sylvester didn't do any more filling in. Their presence spurred reports that it wasn't expedience but Sylvester's ego that had prompted him to direct, and he experienced an uncomfortable sense of déjà vu; it was just a few days into a new film, and already he was being pictured as a bad boy.

However, that was a minor brouhaha compared with what was to follow.

A significant part of the action in *Nighthawks* takes place on the aerial tramway where Wulfgar holds a carload of passengers hostage. The tramway selected by the filmmakers is one that connects Manhattan to Roosevelt Island, a residential strip nestled in the middle of the East River. When filming was announced, a group of residents got up in arms about the inconvenience it would cause, and they decided to go after more money than Universal had agreed to pay. One of the residents, a minister, went so far as to demand that the shoot be canceled altogether because he didn't approve of the script.

Much to the surprise of the crew, the residents managed to get a court injunction and filming was closed down. Though the money the delay cost wasn't coming out of his pocket, Sylvester arranged to meet with the group to see if he could smooth the situation over. Instead of appreciating his efforts at mediation, the residents castigated Sylvester for siding with the studio. Rocky was supposed to stand up for the little guy, not big business.

In the end, the courts found against the Roosevelt Island group, going out of its way to chastise the minister. Poll quoted the judge as saying, "We're not a fascist society. There are laws against censorship." However, the studio did agree to put up $20,000 toward a youth recreation center on the island and also promised to be off the tram and out of everyone's way by rush hour each morning and night.

The converging pressures of breaking up with Anton and being sniped at again by the public and by the press quickly took their toll on Sylvester. He became depressed and began eating a lot, quickly sailing beyond his already hefty *Rocky II* weight of 205. Giving up on exercise, he concurrently lost muscle definition and found himself in the worst physical condition of his life. He also wasn't sleeping well and, because he was still on the outs with his wife, had no one to talk to about his problems. That made his depression even worse and forged a cycle of mental and physical decline. It didn't show in his performance, which was intense and energetic, but Sylvester Stallone was hurting more than at any point in his post-*Rocky* career.

Sylvester's personal problems aside, the shoot itself was calmer than most in the actor's career. Billy Dee Williams admits that Sylvester had "strong ideas which weren't always accepted on the set," but he is quick to add that they "got along great and had lots of fun" and that he found the star "a perfectionist, quite brilliant."

Hauer was slightly less laudatory, but with a reason: he and Sylvester are both extremely intense actors, and they found themselves in competition to see who could generate more electricity on the screen. Hauer says he found the competition "normal and healthy," though he adds that it was also extremely draining.

Unfortunately, the making of the picture was just the relative calm before the storm. After the shoot ended the real shooting started—a virtual replay of the conflict that had raged over *F.I.S.T.*

When Sylvester saw the film, he felt that it focused too heavily on the sociopathic Wulfgar and too little on the police. The terrorist's vicious activities do indeed get a lot of screen time. *Nighthawks* opens with

Wulfgar blowing up a crowded department store in London (children die, we are told), then returns to him repeatedly as he guns down a cringing accomplice at a party, razes a building on Wall Street, murders an airline stewardess, shoots a patron at a crowded disco, takes an old woman hostage during the subway chase, cuts open Fox's face, guns down a young woman in the tram and dumps her body 250 feet into the river, and finally tries to knife Irene in her apartment, only to find that it's DaSilva in drag, the decoy cop promptly shooting several big red holes in the terrorist.

In contrast, there are only two scenes of Sylvester in action as a cop before he meets Wulfgar, and, remarkably, more screen time is devoted to Wulfgar and Shakka together than to Deke and Irene.

To Sylvester, this emphasis was morally wrong, and he protested, though he found it virtually impossible to convince many people that he wasn't complaining because he'd been deprived of screen time, but because he simply didn't like seeing so much of the villain.

Since producer Poll didn't want his picture to go the way of *F.I.S.T.*, he prepared a second version of the film, one in which there was more footage of Sylvester and less of Hauer. Reportedly, the original version was better received by preview audiences, so Malmuth's cut was the one Universal released.

For the record, Sylvester didn't regard this test as any more conclusive than the *F.I.S.T.* screening and has always disliked the industry's reliance on sneak previews. "They can be terribly misleading," he said. He feels there is no such thing as a perfectly representative audience and believes that filmmakers should simply hash out the aesthetics among themselves.

Objectively speaking, the film is actually quite good as is. Grim though they may be, the scenes showing Wulfgar at work are tense and build an unmerciful antagonist for Sylvester. Having said that, stressing Wulfgar's atrocities also makes the picture so relentlessly dark and dreary that its chances at the box office were iffy at best. And sure enough, when the picture opened in April of 1981, it received generally cool reviews and dismal grosses. *Nighthawks* did even worse than *F.I.S.T.* While Sylvester would always wonder, once again, whether his concept would have fared better at the box office, what bothered him more was that after putting himself back on top of the box office heap with *Rocky II,* he had plunged back down again.

More than anything else, Sylvester didn't want to believe that Rocky was the only part in which he would be accepted. However, even before *Nighthawks* had been released, he realized that DaSilva had been enough of a departure so that he'd be wise to venture back into athletics for his next effort. In June of 1980, he went to Hungary to film the wartime soccer story *Escape to Victory,* released simply as *Victory*.

*Victory* is the story of a group of Allied prisoners of war who are forced to play a soccer match against the German national team. The match is arranged to take place before 50,000 Frenchmen in occupied Paris, the Nazi command feeling that an Allied defeat at their hands would serve to fuel the German propaganda machine. The POWs pretend to go along with the game, intending to escape from their captors while they're at the stadium. Naturally, they become so caught up in the match that they abandon their plan, sticking around to beat their swaggering adversaries. It all works out for the best, however, as the players manage to sneak out when the virulently anti-German crowd goes wild over the Allied victory.

Sylvester was compelled to take the part of Hatch not only because "the last twenty minutes of the film are like the fight in *Rocky* with the underdog going for the big fella," but because he'd be working with legendary director John Huston, who had made such classics as *The Maltese Falcon* and *The African Queen*. Hungry for critical success, Sylvester had every reason to believe that, if nothing else, he would be making a film that would at least be an artistic triumph. He was also delighted with the stature of his co-stars, who included Michael Caine as Captain Colby, Max von Sydow as the German propaganda officer Von Steiner, and eighteen of the world's most famous soccer players, among them Brazil's Pélé, England's Bobby Moore, and Ardiles of Argentina.

Unlike his other films, in which only the exteriors were shot on location, all of the $15 million *Victory* was filmed in Hungary. The Gensdorf Prison set was built on the grounds of the Allag Riding Stables outside of Budapest, while the huge MTK Stadium was used to represent Paris's Colombes Stadium. Interior sets were all constructed at Mafilm Studio in Budapest, and more than 250,000 Hungarian extras were employed during the picture's fifty-three-day shoot.

The combination of wanting a hit, being on a foreign

location for so long, and working with Huston, whom
he trusted implicitly, made Sylvester the zenith of
cooperation on *Victory*. Sylvester admits that it wasn't
easy. "Once you've directed, you want to constantly
suggest things." However, as Huston said during the
course of filming, "I'd heard about Sly's reputation for
throwing his weight around, but his behavior here has
been as modest as one could hope for. He couldn't be
more disciplined."

So *Victory* was pleasant for the goodwill on the set
as well as for the fact that Sasha came to Budapest and
the couple was able to put their marriage back together. However, that didn't mean the picture was like
a day at the beach for Sylvester. Not thrilling in the
least was the revelation that a soccer film could be as
debilitating as a boxing picture. He said he thought
that playing a goalie would be simple, but by August
he was describing himself as a "walking blood clot. So
far, I've broken one finger, the others are bent, and
I've had injections and water removed from both
knees. It's just incredible, a very tough sport."

Most of his injuries were sustained while "leaping to
the ground at full speed, with no concern about physical safety and with total concentration on the ball." It
was the way real goalkeepers play, and, as he had
done especially in *Rocky II,* Sylvester didn't want to
fake anything. It would have been bad for the movie
and even worse for his pride.

The physical aspect of the film was made tougher,
Sylvester concedes, because he stayed in character by
living on a "prisoner-of-war diet. That's 900 calories a
day with liquids of any kind, pure protein foods, and

fresh vegetables. Then, every third day, a baked potato for carbohydrates and to keep my brain from turning to fudge." He went home in September having lost the weight he'd put on during *Nighthawks* plus having fallen 26 pounds below his standard weight of 185.

Sylvester also used the making of the film as an excuse to get back into shape. After *Nighthawks,* he had realized that his view of what made a man physically appealing was no longer valid, specifically "that big, strong, bullish look that I'd grown up with." Now he wanted to change that in his own appearance, which he did by adopting a rigorous daily exercise routine that included 300 situps, jumping rope, and lifting weights. The only exercise he had to avoid were pushups because they put a great deal of strain on his mending pectoral muscle. However, less than five months after the surgery he was back doing those as well—the brutal one-armed kind which had impressed audiences during the training scenes in both Rocky movies. Being out of shape soon became utterly loathsome to him, and he decided that the last thing he ever wanted to become again was someone "coated in fat, a human pork chop with a face that's caving in, with eyes like a couple of raisins stuck at the end of a tunnel."

Yet of all Sylvester's experiences, good and bad, nothing was quite so extraordinary as being in Hungary itself. He said during shooting, "Budapest is so alien to me. It's a very lonely place, and I feel great empathy with these people. The police have keys to everyone's house; they can turn off all the electricity in a city if they don't like what's going on. And every couple of months the tanks run down the streets, just to remind people that they're there." Afterwards, he added to his list of complaints, "To this day, I believe all our hotel rooms were bugged. If you had an amorous night with your wife, you'd walk downstairs next morning and everyone would be grinning."

Tangentially, Sylvester tried to use the opportunity of being in Eastern Europe to take a trip into the Soviet Union. However, he says, "they wouldn't give me the clearance" because, he felt, the Rocky films advocated the triumph of the spirit against adversity. And that was something that wouldn't be acceptable to a society where, according to Sylvester, people are fed propaganda "from the time you brush your teeth till the time you brush 'em again."

Not that he needed to visit Russia to realize what he had in the U.S. Hungary alone did that, and it was to have a dramatic impact on the course of his career. He had never regarded himself as politically left or right, just as someone who "loves his country." However, spurred by the oppression he saw in Hungary, he began looking for a way to express that in film. And just as his quest for a hero had given birth to Rocky, so this renewed sense of patriotism would eventually lead him to his second great hero, a Vietnam veteran by the name of John J. Rambo.

# Chapter

## Eleven

Sylvester returned home with high hopes that *Victory* would put an end to his non-Rocky jinx. As it turned out, it would do just the opposite. *Victory* opened to the worst reviews of any Stallone film ever and earned even less money than *Paradise Alley*. Moreover, it wasn't just a case of the critics sniping at Sylvester; *Victory* truly was an awful picture, arguably the most plodding, implausible, and badly written film Huston or any other first-class director has ever made. Even Sylvester's performance lacked energy, and the tedium was relieved only by the superlative stunts by the soccer stars, particularly Pele performing some astonishing over-the-head kicks.

Now, of course, Sylvester had a real problem. Not

only hadn't the public accepted him as something of an intellectual in *Nighthawks*, but they'd rejected him as an athlete in *Victory*. He couldn't have come closer to a character and a story like *Rocky*, yet he'd been rebuffed in no uncertain terms.

Scripts were still being submitted to him, but Sylvester knew he couldn't accept any of them. The industry and the press were once again tagging him as a loser, and studios are reluctant to put advertising money behind a movie starring a has-been. Since that's the kiss of death for a film, and since another commercial failure or two would have ensured Sylvester's demise as a major star, he chose to make another Rocky picture before trying anything else.

Though it made sense intellectually, it was a difficult decision for Sylvester to accept emotionally, and he spent a lot of time alone, behind the wheel of his favorite car, a cherry red '56 Chevy Impala, puffing reflectively on his pipe as he drove around town or through the hills.

On the one hand, he knew another Rocky picture would make money and give him a few more turns at bat in major motion pictures. On the other hand, it would obviously tie him even closer to the Rocky persona, something he'd previously admitted that he found "abhorrent" because he "wanted to be respected as an intellectual and an earthshaker." He says that he couldn't even escape the part when he went to the White House, where President Reagan addressed him not as Sylvester or Sly but as Rocky.

But the double whammy of *Nighthawks* and *Victory* brought back a lot of old fears, and in a moment of extreme candor he told reporter James Verniere, "I don't want to blow what I've got." While he admitted that it was an "inhibiting quality for an artist or an actor to have," he acknowledged that his dual failure had left him feeling considerably "less brave."

Then too, being in Hungary had softened his resentment somewhat. Sylvester had seen how utterly without hope the Hungarian people were, with nothing remotely approaching a Rocky in their lives. When he came home he reminded himself of the reasons he'd created Rocky in the first place and told himself that "there is a tremendous validity in trying to preserve a character that has endeared himself to a cross-section of the viewing audience. Rocky will outlive me, and it's important to make a contribution that lives on longer than the meat hanging off these bones."

However, most important of all in convincing the actor to lace up the gloves yet again was the fact that while he was in Hungary Sylvester had conceived of a way to do a new kind of Rocky, an angle he calls "a godsend."

The actor himself had changed a great deal between *Nighthawks* and *Victory*. He had gone from being an out-of-shape hedonist ("a walking whoopee cushion" is how he describes it) to a trim, cooperative, determined man, and he began writing a screenplay in which Rocky went through that same kind of metamorphosis. It was a master stroke; in that way he could give the public what it wanted, give himself an acting challenge, and, most important of all, win back the critics. By admitting, through Rocky, that they'd been partially right, that he'd been careless, cocky, and complacent, he'd earn not only their respect but their compassion as well.

Thus, while Sylvester would have preferred to play Poe, fulfill a longstanding ambition to make a musical, or do any number of different projects, he ended up agreeing to write, star in, and direct *Rocky III*. He agreed to direct because, despite the havoc it caused at home, he says plaintively, in view of his track record, "I didn't know if I'd ever get the chance to write, direct, and act in the same film again." No doubt, the $10 million ($5 million up front, $1 million per year for five years) plus profit-sharing he was given made the pill easier to swallow, but Sylvester maintains that if he hadn't had a valid story, he would not have done the picture.

According to Sylvester, the essence of *Rocky III* is adaptation. Between *Rocky II* and *Rocky III*, the fighter has become "civilized . . . matured . . . *nouveau riche.*" He lives in a mansion now, with servants and opulence all around him. Unknown to him, he has remained the heavyweight champion primarily because Mickey has set him up with easy opponents. Learning this proves to be a terrible blow to his pride and, to help win back his self-respect, he agrees to fight an ambitious bruiser of a fighter ominously named Clubber Lang. Lang knocks the stuffings out of the Italian Stallion, and it remains for none other than Apollo Creed to whip Rocky back into shape, help him slim down, replace his brawling style with one of finesse, and get back the hungry "eye of the tiger" in order to win back his title.

The regimen Creed puts Rocky through to make him

a leaner, sharper fighter is virtually identical to the kind of torture Sylvester put himself through to make the movie.

When he had begun slimming down in Hungary, Sylvester's mental and emotional state had also improved. He realized then how closely tied the mind and body were and resolved to remake himself when he returned to the U.S.

With seven months before shooting was scheduled to begin on *Rocky III*, Sylvester dropped himself down to 155 pounds "and then began to add in increments of an ounce here and an ounce there. The idea was the reverse of body building. Instead of adding bulk and then sculpting down, I went down and added it on. Everything that was put on was high definition, low fat, and that meant eating just ten egg whites a day, some burnt toast—so there was no water in it—and every third day a piece of fruit." With his penchant for understatement, Sylvester says, "It was bad news." However, the results were not. Instead of the burly figure he'd been in the previous Rocky pictures, the new, improved Sylvester had an impressive 47-inch chest and a trim 29½-inch waist.

Despite the fact that his diet left him "weak and dizzy all the time" (his body-fat level had dropped to 4½ percent, whereas most American males average between 15 percent and 20 percent), Sylvester simultaneously broke in a murderous training routine. He had no choice. In order to master Rocky's new fighting style—which Sylvester describes as going from "wild and bullish to a sophisticated fighting machine"—the actor had to build his own endurance. He says, "To box and dance as Rocky would be doing in the film takes at least ten times the amount of energy it does to plod and slug."

To this end, Sylvester's new routine began with a two-mile jog in the morning, followed by eighteen rounds of sparring, two hours of weightlifting and jumping rope, a short nap, and then a two-mile run—not jogging, but at breakneck speed. He would conclude his regimen with a swim, at which time it was late afternoon and he'd have to begin his day's work on the film—polishing the script, talking with set designers and wardrobe personnel, and casting the new characters who'd be appearing in the picture.

Working with Sylvester in the ring this time around was fifty-year-old Ray Notaro, proprietor and resident expert at the Left Hook Gym. The two had first worked together on *Rocky,* where their relationship went sour when the former professional middleweight began sparring so seriously that Sylvester ended with a set of broken ribs. He didn't go back to Notaro for *Rocky II*. However, since Rocky had to adopt a different style of fighting, Sylvester knew he had to train with the best. He made up with Notaro, and the two worked out at the ring, which was constructed at the studio, Sylvester relishing each new move he learned. In the space of a few short months he'd become such a fanatic about fitness and athletics that he couldn't absorb the new talents fast enough. Indeed, so zealous did Sylvester become that while he and Notaro were sparring one day he broke several of the trainer's ribs. Notaro insists he was thrilled to death despite his pain, proudly claiming that his student was "now as good as any six-round professional fighter." Sylvester was also pleased, though he declared that he wouldn't be happy until he was "able to legitimately go ten rounds."

At the end of the seven months, Sylvester was literally a new man. He looked like Adonis and had regained his own eye of the tiger. Despite his reservations about playing Rocky yet again, he was juiced up and ready to make a picture that would eclipse the others.

His personal enthusiasm notwithstanding, Sylvester knew that one of the keys to making *Rocky III* work was the casting of Clubber Lang. Originally, he had it in mind to cast a boxer for the part, feeling that it would be easier to teach an athlete to act than vice versa. However, he scuttled that idea after "interviewing" heavyweights Earnie Shavers and Joe Frazier . . . in the ring. Says the actor, "Frazier gave me four stitches," while Shavers "made me realize I can't function on this earth without lungs. The instincts of the ring took over, and he nearly knocked mine out my mouth. You want to know what it looked like? Like those cartoons when Tom of Tom and Jerry is slugged by a bulldog or something and just sails, stiff as a board, out of the frame." Sylvester laughs that the first time Shavers hit him in the chest, "I macho-ed it all the way into the men's room before I threw up." After tangling with those two men, he decided to go for an actor instead.

It was casting director Rhonda Young, Sylvester's ally from his New York days, who finally came up with a physical titan who was also a natural ham. In October of 1980, she discovered twenty-eight-year-old, 6-

foot 1-inch bodyguard and bouncer Lawrence Tero (originally Tureaud). Known professionally as Mr. T, he had just won the title of America's Toughest Bouncer for the second year running—a contest that included not only boxing but seeing how far each contestant could throw a stuntperson. Mr. T nonchalantly says of his championship toss, "I picked him up like a barbell . . . let out a gigantic yell and let the stuntman fly through the air. When he landed and the dust cleared, he was lying on the 14-foot mark and I was in first place." Seeing the competition when it was aired on NBC-TV, Rhonda called the champ at his home in Chicago and asked if he would be interested in auditioning for a part in the next Rocky film. He said he'd love to, provided that the part was not that of a pimp or a dope dealer. "I was not the kind of guy who would do anything just to be in a movie," the upright T insists. When told that he'd be auditioning for the part of a boxer, he agreed to the test.

Mr. T was sent a seven-page script extract to study, and he immediately began rehearsing the dialogue for several hours each day, the rest of the time going around muttering things like "I'll bust you up" and "I'll break your arm in six places." More determined than confident, he went to the audition in January set on winning the part, "even if I had to fight Joe Frazier and Earnie Shavers at the same time" to get it.

Mr. T was one of 1500 people trying out for the part, and he was at once nervous but psyched to learn that Sylvester would be present for his screen test. However, Mr. T reports that the star couldn't have been more accommodating. "He pulled me over to a corner and said, 'If you make a mistake, we'll do it again.' He told me to relax."

That, of course, was easier said than done. Apart from a case of nerves, Mr. T had to contend with having a woman feed him Rocky's lines. The situation didn't exactly reek of verisimilitude, but Mr. T did so well (he says modestly, "Sly was so impressed that he could hardly say 'Cut'") that Sylvester ended the screen test after four pages and came over to try some improvisation. Following that short exercise, Mr. T was asked to get mad for the cameras. He whistled up the kind of anger he'd practiced at home and did a terrific take—if he does say so himself. "I was just super," he says. "I amazed myself."

When Mr. T was finished, Sylvester told him that it had been a great audition and they'd let him know within a week whether the part was his. Mr. T thanked him for the opportunity just to have participated and went home unable to do anything but think about what he'd done and whether it had been enough. He got his answer four days later when Rhonda Young called. In spite of what Sylvester called "some pretty tough competition," the part was his. Mr. T reveals that he was so thrilled he "couldn't wait to tell somebody." Unfortunately, he was also "so excited and happy" that he "couldn't remember their numbers to save my life."

Once he'd signed aboard, Mr. T's regimen was as brutal as Sylvester's. Not only did he have to build up his muscles, but Sylvester wanted him to shed roughly 20 of his 230 pounds. To this end, he'd wake at 6:00 a.m. 7 days a week, run 5 miles, do situps and pushups until he ached, then go back to sleep until 10:00 a.m. At noon, he would awaken and have lunch, followed by two hours of boxing with Sylvester, during which time they'd work out the moves they'd be doing in the film. "Miss a step and you're in for a detached retina," Sylvester warned the newcomer, stressing the importance of sticking to the "very precise choreography." Once again, Sylvester wanted a fight that would be infinitely more exciting than the one that had come before it. He worked it out so that there were 130 separate punches as opposed to the 75 in *Rocky II* and the "mere" 35 from *Rocky*.

The boxing rehearsal would end at about 4:00; then Mr. T would hone his boxing skills by working out on the heavy bag and the speed bag, after which he'd jump rope and shadowbox. Sylvester was so impressed with his find that just before the picture was about to roll, he said at a press conference, "You don't rehearse Mr. T; you just turn him loose!"

It was a pronouncement that had more truth to it than Sylvester realized. When they finally got down to filming the fight before 6000 screaming extras, Sylvester says Mr. T got so "caught up in the reality of the moment that there were moments when I was overcome with real fear. When the pounding was over, I ached for weeks."

Sylvester was ready, Mr. T was ready, and in April of 1981 the Rocky cast reassembled. The sole absentee was Butkus, who had died shortly before. Though he was replaced at home by the mastiff Rocky and the terrier Attila, his part was not filled in the film. However, added to the ranks from the Stallone household was Sage, who played a small role as Rocky Jr.

Sylvester finished the picture in two months, which was an impressive achievement considering the number of fight scenes, not to mention location shooting in both Los Angeles and Philadelphia. Mr. T marveled, "Imagine that, three months' training but only eight weeks to film!"

But speed and quality are not interrelated in Stallone productions. He says, "I *like* to work fast," and with a clear vision of exactly the kind of film he wanted to make and a budget nearly twice that of the previous Rocky films combined, he created what was to be the most sprawling, thrilling, and successful film of the series—and, for Sylvester, the most terrifying as well.

# Chapter

## Twelve

Sylvester's attitude toward movie sequels hadn't changed since *Rocky II*. He still felt they were a valid art form, particularly in light of the soul-searching he'd done to come up with a story for *Rocky III*. However, more tolerant than he'd been three years before, Sylvester said that he understood how they'd gotten a bad reputation and fully expected his new film to take a critical licking.

"Unfortunately," he said, "many filmmakers have gone after only the money, and it's left a bad taste in people's mouths. So I expect the critics to go into theaters with their pencils sharpened and a chip on their shoulder." He threw up his hands. "I would." Statements such as these may not have been contrived to soften the critics, but they didn't hurt.

Yet what really won them over and earned Sylvester his most favorable reviews since *Rocky* was Sylvester's candor and deftness in showing how success had brought Rocky/Stallone down. *Time* magazine said of the film that Sylvester had put "satin trunks on his autobiography," and while the picture had much more going for it than that, critics enjoyed seeing Sylvester baring his soul.

It also helped that the picture had a do-or-die quality for its backer, MGM. The studio had bought United Artists between Rockys and was choking on debt, what with the cost of the purchase and a series of expensive flops like Steve Martin's *Pennies from Heaven, Cannery Row,* and the Marlon Brando–George C. Scott disaster *The Formula*. With the fate of the venerable old studio on the line, critics went out of their way to be kinder than usual.

However, even with all these peripheral assets, the picture could not have won critical or public acclaim without the heart and action that had become synonymous with the Rocky saga—and *Rocky III* had those in heart-pounding abundance. Apart from the two thrilling bouts with Clubber Lang, there's the seething hatred that exists between Lang and Apollo Creed; a training sequence that works up more sweat per frame than either of the earlier Rockys; a terrific exhibition match in which Rocky battles the towering wrestler Thunderlips (played by 6-foot 6-inch wrestler Hulk Hogan), a sequence inspired by an impromptu contest that occurred in 1974 when Muhammad Ali climbed into the ring with wrestler Gorilla Monsoon; and a heart-rending scene in which trainer Mickey gets so worked up before the first fight with Lang that he subsequently dies in Rocky's arms.

*Rocky III* would have been even more of a tearjerker if Sylvester had gone with his original idea. He reveals, "I wanted him to fight his heart out so much that on the way home in the car, he puts his head on his wife's shoulder and whispers, 'I'm so tired. Can I use your shoulder a second?' And he dies. He fought until his heart is shattered. Of course," Sylvester sighs, "you'd have a movie that would totally go down the toilet, but that's what I wanted."

So Rocky lived, not only in the film but in the box office as well. The picture opened in May of 1982, and before *Rocky III* ended its run late that year it had returned nearly $66 million to MGM/UA, an incredible 20 percent more than *Rocky* had made. That doesn't even include the licensing, which not only included magazines and bubble gum cards but action figures, posters, a top-selling Colecovision videogame, and other paraphernalia.

Indeed, one of the *Rocky III* tie-ins went a long way toward helping the movie become the success it was: the chart-topping theme song from the picture, "Eye of the Tiger." Demographically, teenagers compose both rock music's biggest audience and the largest share of the moviegoing public. Thus, a hit song increases awareness of the picture and can add millions to the box office. In the case of *Rocky III,* this energy was a reward Sylvester richly deserved because he took a chance and gave an unknown band named Survivor the opportunity to write and record the song.

Sylvester recalls that after he'd finished shooting the

picture, "I was sitting in a friend's office and heard a group on a tape. I said, 'Boy, they're really good.' And my friend told me that this group had been trying to get off the ground for a long time but that they just couldn't find the right hook. Well," he says, "I sent Survivor a videotape of *Rocky III*, told them I needed a theme song, and three days later they sent me 'Eye of the Tiger.' "

Though Sylvester had also commissioned songs from established writers, he used the one by Survivor because "these kids were hungry and eager" and he admired that. That kind of generosity is typical of Sylvester, and it's worth noting how many of the participants from *Rocky III* have gone on to stardom. Survivor remains a popular group, their most recent album *Vital Signs* having gone platinum in the summer of 1985; Hulk Hogan is a multi-million-dollar draw on the pro-wrestling circuit; and Mr. T, of course, is a regular on the hit series "The A-Team.'

Apart from being a starmaker, *Rocky III* was also a film that showed Sylvester that at thirty-five it was perhaps a little easier to be a philanthropist than a gymnast. He'd always prided himself on not having had any personal heroes since childhood because, he says, "for someone to be my hero, he has to be able to do something that I feel never in a million years would I be able to do. But you couldn't tell me that, because I would keep on trying. My goals become so high that, no matter what I have in the icebox, I'm still clawing."

Perhaps no person could tell Sylvester that certain things were beyond him, but he became a rapt audience when his body started talking.

The last scene Sylvester had to shoot for the film

was part of the training sequence, a demanding take which goes through a vigorous swimming routine. Just before he finished, Sylvester went into shock, trembling and breathing rapidly as he struggled to reach the side of the pool. Helped from the water, he was stretched out on a towel, where his skin went white and his body temperature plummeted.

"My heart was doing 210 beats a minute," he says with a shiver, "and the paramedics gave me oxygen, carried me to bed, covered me in ice, then wrapped me in towels." Sylvester was extremely nauseated but conscious, and he acknowledges, "That was the only time in my life that I was *really* frightened. My body seemed to be saying, 'I can't take it anymore, Stallone, you've pushed me to the limit. I quit.''

But Stallone, being Stallone, didn't quit. If anything, having his body revolt like that only seemed to strengthen his resolve to make it do what he wanted. He got up as soon as he could to begin editing his movie, explaining to his doctors and his wife that he simply couldn't live any other way.

His body would more or less put up with Sylvester's stubbornness through two extremely demanding action pictures, *First Blood* and *Rambo: First Blood, Part II*. However, in the spring of 1985, the star's luck would once again run out, and he'd end up putting himself back in the hospital while working on—what else?—*Rocky IV*.

Aside from his illness, the only genuinely unpleasant memory he has of *Rocky III* is a fiasco involving the statue of Rocky seen in the film.

In the first two pictures, Rocky runs up the sixty-eight steps of the Philadelphia Art Museum and, reaching the landing, holds his arms aloft in triumph. In *Rocky III,* the city recognizes this tradition by unveiling an 8½-foot-tall bronze statue in honor of their favorite son. Arms held high on a 5-foot pedestal, the statue becomes a permanent fixture on the landing in the film.

Since his films had done more to popularize Philadelphia than anything since cream cheese, Sylvester thought it would be an appropriate gesture to give the city the 800-pound, $60,000 sculpture and to have them leave it in front of the museum. He reasoned that not only would it be a fitting tribute to Rocky and the city, but tourists were sure to flock to the museum to see it, even more tourists than the thousands who already made the pilgrimage each year to run up the stairs. As *People* magazine wrote, "After all, everyone knows how that other large bronze casting in town, the Liberty Bell, draws tourists."

However, the museum balked at Sylvester's generosity, one board member huffing, "What great institution has an *illustration* in front of it?" Sylvester was nonplussed; after all, no one who visited *his* home seemed bothered by the fact that he had a Rodin sculpture sitting near a boxer's headguard inscribed "To Sly from Muhammad Ali." Denver sculptor A. Thomas Schomberg, who had taken eight months to create the work, was also annoyed, and shot back that the bronze would not be at all out of place in front of the Grecian structure. But the Philadelphia Art Commission refused to reconsider the edict, and the statue was shipped back to Los Angeles, where it sat, lashed to a tree like Odysseus, in Sylvester's yard.

Meanwhile, in a very Rockyesque development, a

group of blue-collar Philadelphians, upset by the ruling, got together to try and change the city's mind. They went to the media, circulated petitions, and forced Philadelphia's City Commission to ask for the statue back and find it a suitable home. What they finally settled on was the Spectrum, home of the Flyers hockey team and 76ers basketball team and the site of many historic boxing matches. Sylvester agreed to the stadium site, and as something of a face-saving gesture to everyone concerned, the city allowed the statue to stand at the art museum for the first two months the picture was in release.

Given all the reasons not to have done *Rocky III,* Sylvester came out of it with much more than he'd expected. Not only had he proven that Rocky was still a draw, but he'd pulled in new fans, people who saw him with his slimmer, more muscular physique and more angular matinee-idol face. And in portraying Rocky as less of a lug, he showed his largest audience to date that he was an *actor.*

In the same stroke, he'd proven to Hollywood once and for all that he was a triple-threat filmmaker. The script crackled with invention, the requisite clichés were well used, and the dialogue was at once witty and warm. And he'd directed the picture quickly and relatively inexpensively, yet gave it a remarkably slick and polished look (unlike the dark, often stolid *Rocky II* and especially *Paradise Alley*).

Past failures were forgotten by the public and by the industry, and in the words of one of Sylvester's representatives, "people lined up to do business with him."

In an interesting postscript to the phenomenon of *Rocky III,* people also lined up to do business *without* him. Shortly after the release of *Rocky III*, there was a spate of Sylvester Stallone lookalikes partying at Hollywood nightspots and running up huge tabs. Feeling sorry for the proprietors who'd been "bilked out of money," Sylvester told the press that he was considering holding an open call for lookalikes in order to round them up. The scam came to an abrupt end.

After *Rocky III* had finished shooting but more than half a year before it was released, Sylvester was still unsure about how it would be received. He was still preoccupied with the desire to have a hit "without gloves" and remained on the lookout for appropriate properties. In the wake of Hungary and the lingering pain of the Iranian hostage situation, he was also still hoping to find a picture that would make a positive statement about Americans. That was when aspiring producers Andrew Vajna and Mario Kassar came to him with a project called *Blood Knot*, a film that was eventually released as *First Blood*. And whether it's karma or coincidence, once again a Stallone project got off the ground with a Rocky-like bucking of the odds.

*First Blood*, based on a novel by David Morell, is the story of a Vietnam veteran who is wronged by the law and goes on a defensive, psychotic killing spree. Originally published in 1972, it was optioned almost immediately for a movie. However, after a script was written, the project sat on Warner Brothers' shelf for ten years, the studio having second thoughts and deciding that no one would want to see a movie about a homicidal veteran.

Early in 1982, distributors Vajna and Kassar were

trying to break into motion picture production. Their expertise was as foreign sales agents, and, though they'd helped to raise money for films in the past, they wanted to be able to produce a picture that was tailor-made for both the U.S. and international markets.

Since action pictures do enormously well overseas, especially in markets such as the Far East and the Philippines, they went through studio vaults to find unproduced scripts. They found *First Blood* and bought it, feeling that the script could be toned down.

The matter of casting was crucial to the project, since very few stars could act convincingly in an action film and at the same time have sufficient box-office clout to attract investors and, later, generate big-money sales to cable, cassette, and network TV. Burt Reynolds and Clint Eastwood were too old to play Vietnam veterans, suitable stars like Richard Gere and William Hurt were into art, and actors who had done pictures of this type tended to be shallow musclemen without much range.

Given the success of the Rocky films around the world and the positive scuttlebutt about *Rocky III,* the producers decided that Sylvester was the actor best qualified to make the film. They offered him a whopping $3.5 million to star and granted him the standard provision that he be allowed to tailor the character to himself and, more important, find a way to make him more human. This fit in perfectly with Sylvester's game plan. He didn't need an acting tour de force just then; he needed a non-Rocky box office hit. He liked the fact that *First Blood* had the kind of "heavy action

[that] people want today in films," and he accepted the part, though he made it clear from the start that he had no interest in directing the film as well. As he later told Ted Kotcheff, the man who got the job, "I'm *tired* of making decisions. I just want to act."

The screenplay, as rewritten, achieved a delicate balance, changing the character from, in Sylvester's words, "a psychopath [who] killed everybody" to someone who not only disdained killing (the only death he causes is accidental) but who actually tries to stop the hostilities at several points during the story, only to be rebuffed by the police. Director Ted Kotcheff elaborated, "It's not so much that he loses control, but that he reverts to a way of living over which he has complete control—guerrilla warfare. His training has given him an almost mystical connection with nature."

The finished script is the story of John Rambo, a former Green Beret and Congressional Medal of Honor winner. Disconsolate when he learns that his last surviving army buddy has died, he wanders into the backwater town of Holidayland to find a place to eat. Looking rather bedraggled, he is told to leave town; when he refuses, he is arrested by the local police. When the officers try to shave him with a straight-edge razor, Rambo flashes back to his days as a POW when he was tortured with a razor. Going berserk, he turns his martial arts skills on the officers, breaking noses and sternums, escaping, stealing weapons and a motorcycle, and holing up in a nearby wooded mountain area. As Sylvester succinctly puts

it, he "reverts back to the warrior and it becomes a
one-man survival course," waging war against Police
Chief Teasle (Brian Dennehy) and his men. To his
credit, Rambo never kills men on purpose, preferring
to cripple them with bullets in the legs, sharpened
stakes in the groin, rifle butts in the belly, and nooses
around the neck. As he tells Teasle when he briefly
holds the officer prisoner, "In town, you're the law;
out here, it's me. Don't push it."

To assist the hapless law officer, Green Beret Colonel Sam Trautman (Richard Crenna), Rambo's former
commanding officer, arrives on the scene. His advice
isn't heeded, of course ("I'm gonna pin that Medal of
Honor to his liver," vows the mortified Teasle), and
Rambo survives everything from a helicopter attack to
a fall from a cliff to a mine explosion. Ultimately, he
snatches an army truck and, after crashing it into a gas
station, shoots up the police station and explodes a
gun shop. Then, while Main Street burns to the
ground, Rambo goes after Teasle. He shoots but does
not kill the police chief—more or less evening the
score in his mind—and, rather than continue the fight,
allows himself to be captured.

In the novel, Rambo dies, killed by Trautman, which
is how the filmmakers originally intended to end their
picture. However, looking at the finished movie they
decided that it was not only unsatisfactory but obviously precluded a sequel. Bringing back Sylvester and
sundry cast members, they shot the ending as it now
stands.

As with all his films, Sylvester went into *First Blood*

after a lot of preparation. Only this time it wasn't just physical training, such as studying with a former Green Beret advisor to learn survival tactics and hand-to-hand combat. He also did a lot of psychological homework, spending time in veterans hospitals, talking with former soldiers about how they'd reacted to the dual problems of stress under fire and the public's disdain for what they'd done in Vietnam. Sylvester may not use many words in the picture, but his research is all there on the screen. Before he's arrested the first time, there's a lot of anger beneath the surface, anger the actor had seen in the eyes of so many forgotten veterans. In fact, he was so moved by their plight that after he finished making the film he did a great deal of work with the Vietnam Veterans of America, doing benefits and making countless personal appearances, long before it was fashionable. As he put it, "There are a lot of vets who will hang on to every word in this film, so I can't just be frivolous and say that this is just a gig."

In addition to Sylvester, the cast included Brian Dennehy as Teasle and Richard Crenna as the straight-laced Trautman. Originally, Kirk Douglas had been signed to play Rambo's ex-commander, and he would have been superb, having played similar military figures in *Seven Days in May* and *The Final Countdown*, among other films. However, he left the picture after several days' shooting when it became clear that his concept of the character was incompatible with the shooting script, in which his part was little more than an extended cameo.

Kotcheff explains, "Kirk signed on the condition that his role would be modified, made more important. He took my word, and I tried very hard to extend Trautman's scenes. Sylvester worked on various approaches too." Shooting began without the problem having been resolved, and Douglas finally agreed that he would play the script as written if, in Kotcheff's words, "we could give him the climax." To do that would have meant depriving Rambo of a scene-stealing monologue in which he breaks down and cries over his lost buddies. As Kotcheff realized, "there was no way Kirk and Sylvester could share that moment, dramatically." The director told *Prevue* magazine, "I had to tell Kirk that we couldn't give him the strong scene he deserved, and we parted. It wasn't his fault. He was paid, but I know he was a little angry and disappointed." Kotcheff adds that he even waited a few days before considering a replacement, hoping that Douglas would change his mind. But it didn't happen and, remembering the superb performance Crenna had given in *Body Heat,* he hired a new Trautman.

Needless to say, Sylvester was extremely disappointed. He stated that the star of *The Vikings* "was one of my childhood heroes, and I was looking forward to working with him." However, aware of reports in the press that his ego was once again to blame, Sylvester was quick to add, "His leaving had nothing to do with me."

Given Douglas's departure and how much went wrong with the film, it's miraculous that the picture would end up running only three weeks over schedule. One crew member equated the making of the film to actually fighting a war, and while Sylvester didn't suffer anything quite so debilitating as shock, he deserved the equivalent of a Medal of Honor for the hardships he did endure.

# Chapter

## Thirteen

The $16 million *First Blood* was filmed from November through January in and around Hope, British Columbia, and there were problems literally from day one.

Foremost among these were Sylvester's injuries. Among the first scenes shot for the film was one in which Rambo jumps from the side of a cliff into a tree. A stunt actor did the long shot of the 100-foot drop, leaving only the close-up for Sylvester. However, falling 4 feet into an uncushioned tree can be hazardous as well. Shooting the scene cost Sylvester four broken ribs, and when he thuds against the biggest of the limbs, the crack is nearly audible in the film. After a doctor had bandaged the actor up, Sylvester slipped back into his parka and filming was resumed.

The next accident wasn't as serious, though it could well have cost Sylvester a few fingers. In the scene, Sylvester had to run into an abandoned mine followed by a volley of gunfire. The special effects technician was given precise instructions about when to set off the charges simulating bullets which had been planted in the mine. However, he triggered them a few seconds before Sylvester hit his mark. One of the explosives went off in a beam just inches from where the actor had placed his hand for support. His palm and thumb were badly burned, though no one knew about it until the scene was finished. A scream rang out from the darkness of the mine, and crew members ran over. Sylvester got his second trip to the hospital.

Sylvester made his third trip to the infirmary shortly thereafter when he was hurt stealing the motorcycle to make his getaway. While wrestling off the stunt actor, he cracked a vertebra and badly pulled a back muscle. However, as the next few days of shooting required him "simply" to sling around a 40-pound machine gun, filming was not halted.

Sylvester later joked that in spite of all the injuries he received and running around half naked in a numbing Canadian winter, the only time he ended up in bed was when he finally returned to Los Angeles, felled by a cold.

Nor was Sylvester the only one hurt on *First Blood*. Dennehy cracked three ribs when he did the close-up of his fall through a skylight and also suffered a badly cut hand while filming a fight with Sylvester, the latter wielding his menacing 15-inch hunting knife. The customized $2000 knife also slashed Sylvester during one scene when he jammed it into its sheath, the sharpened blade actually slicing through the leather and scoring the actor.

Among the stuntpeople, the worst injury anyone suffered was while filming the scene in which Teasle's police car jumps over a railroad crossing in hot pursuit of Rambo on his motorcycle. The driver hit the specially constructed ramps a bit faster than he should have, jumping the vehicle 150 feet, three times longer than planned. When the car landed, the stunt actor suffered several collapsed vertebrae and ended up in traction.

Happily, no one was hurt shooting the film's most dangerous stunt, a 150-foot fall from a moving helicopter. Conditions couldn't have been worse. The stunt actor did the drop in a narrow gorge with the helicopter fighting powerful updrafts. His target was an airbag which, according to action coordinator Conrad Tomasano, "looks like a postage stamp from that height." But the stunt went without a hitch, proving the Hollywood adage that it's usually the relatively simple scenes in which people are hurt.

As much as the action in the film caused injuries, it never cost the crew a single day of shooting. Only the weather did that. Says Crenna, "We shot in the worst weather in the area's history." Not only was it unseasonably cold—which is saying something for the Canadian northwest—but there were inordinate amounts of snow and freezing rain. That repeatedly shut down the production and made the stunts more dangerous because of rain-slickened cliffs and sets.

Of everyone working on the film, Crenna was probably the least concerned by the delays, since his contract stipulated that he was to receive a hefty pay increase if the production ran over schedule. When it became clear that the weather was going to be uncooperative, shooting was rescheduled and all of Crenna's scenes were done up front, enabling him to go home on time.

Certainly the oddest problem the filmmakers faced was the theft of $50,000 worth of weapons late in January. Worth twice that on the black market, the forty-seven guns were taken from wooden cases stored inside a 5-ton truck. Although there were two padlocks on each of the side doors and a combination lock in the rear, there was no sign of forced entry, nor was anyone untoward seen or heard by soldiers from the Canadian Army, who were playing extras in the film and allegedly watching the truck at all times. Though the M-16 rifles, magnums, shotguns, and the rest had all been changed so that they fired only blanks, altering them back would not be difficult. The professionalism of the crime, as well as the fact that none of the fifty realistic-looking dummy guns had been stolen, convinced officials of the Royal Canadian Mounted Police that gunrunners were responsible for the theft. As Kotcheff summed it up, "The operation was perfect and the guns are probably on their way to Northern Ireland or Lebanon."

As trying as the filming of *First Blood* had been, getting it into theaters proved almost as difficult for the producers. Despite Sylvester's presence in the picture, few distributors were offering the kind of deal they were after. Universal offered $4 million up front

for the rights to distribution but that included the
lucrative television rights; Paramount and Warner
Brothers made similar offers. But the producers
wanted *only* to sell theatrical distribution rights, and
these eventually went to Sylvester's old United Artists
ally Mike Medavoy, who had since cofounded the
fledgling Orion Pictures. As Medavoy told reporter
Eric Kasum, "It's entertaining and Sylvester is great
in it. We think it will do very well." Orion put up no
front money but agreed to spend $5 million on adver-
tising, leaving TV, foreign, and home video rights with
the filmmakers.

Sylvester shared their optimism, though he admits
that there were some frantic moments when they
started putting together all of the footage they'd
filmed. The Reagan-inspired patriotism that would
soon sweep the country had not yet taken hold, and
Sylvester said that while "there's been a big change in
the country's mood, we didn't know that *then*. When
we looked at the footage, we were scared to death."
Scenes were cut to make Rambo seem less savage. For
example, the murder of several tracking dogs is simply
alluded to in dialogue. But by October of 1982, when
the picture opened, audiences proved that they were
ready for an aggressive war hero, and the picture
returned a hefty $25 million to the producers in the
U.S. alone, collecting an incredible $100 million inter-
nationally. With *Rocky III* still in release, the second
half of 1982 truly belonged to Sylvester Stallone.

As an actor, Sylvester did a splendid job on *First
Blood*. The transformation from an eager, smiling

young man as he looks up his army buddy, to a numbed, angry husk when he learns of his friend's death is accomplished with subtlety and sensitivity. The subsequent transition from this state of shock to feral rage is equally well done, and as a cool killing machine Sylvester is like Charles Bronson cut from steel.

Yet in no scene is Sylvester more effective than when he finally breaks down at the end, actually hugging Colonel Trautman for support. More than any other scene, the climax captures the pain and solitude of the character and the thousands of veterans he represents.

What's most interesting about the Rambo character, however, is that he's really the flip side of Rocky. As rewritten by Sylvester, he's not so much flipped out as unfathomable. Where Rocky is emotional and demonstrative and the viewer always knows what he wants, Rambo (more so in *Rambo: First Blood, Part II*) is for the most part private and unexpressive, rarely revealing his dreams or aspirations.

Not unexpectedly, both of these characters are very much a part of the actor himself. "There are really two Sylvesters living under the same skin," says Kotcheff. "There's one Sylvester who's kind of shy, introspective, intelligent, sensitive, and gentle. The other side is primitive, aggressive, emotional, uncontrollable. Kind of a wild animal, almost. Audiences sense this range and power which makes him unique among contemporary stars." As Kotcheff accurately states it, with Rocky and now Rambo, Sylvester became the modern star most like "the stars of another generation—Cagney and Bogart—who had 'slum' written on their brows, but somehow this was combined with a kind of grace and sensitivity as well."

Obviously, Sylvester was thrilled with the success of *First Blood*. Although Rambo was still an action character and not the stuff of which Oscar nominations are made, it gave him even more leeway in accepting non-Rocky roles. To this end, after finishing the picture, he immediately began looking for something that would stretch his acting muscles.

One of the projects he desperately wanted to film was a story he'd written himself, called *Pals*. Sylvester describes it as "a sort of younger generation *Odd Couple*," a story reportedly based on the years that actors Marlon Brando and Wally Cox had roomed together when they were first starting out. Sylvester, of course, would have taken the Brando part, and he'd hoped to interest someone like Dustin Hoffman or Woody Allen in the Wally Cox role. But that picture was just too far afield for him, and he couldn't get it off the ground, nor could he revive his grim old project *The Bodyguard*.

One project that he came somewhat closer to doing would have been a bold and controversial step for him, a cable-TV version of Tennessee Williams's *A Streetcar Named Desire*. However, he himself finally backed off that one, stating, "It's a haunted play, and there was no way I could win. Everybody would compare my Stanley Kowalski with Marlon Brando's. I felt it would become a race—the 100-yard thespian 'dash.' Who will win, Brando's specter or Stallone?"

Paradoxically, despite *Pals* and *A Streetcar Named Desire,* Sylvester admits that Marlon Brando is not the actor he most admires. That honor goes to Peter O'Toole, of whom Sylvester says, "He's so free! I know this man was probably just out there chasing a script girl, and then when the cameras start rolling he turns on such power. I am in such awe of him!"

With so much potential and so little to do, Sylvester realized that one of his problems was the scattershot nature of his efforts. What he had to do was select *one* studio and establish a multipicture relationship, an arrangement in which he might do a film they wanted to make in exchange for one that he wanted. Taking a cue from Warren Beatty, who had an ongoing relationship with Paramount, Sylvester set up an "overhead deal" with the studio. What this meant was that Paramount would provide him with offices, pay for his secretarial help, and provide money for him to commission screenplays (although the studio did nix the hiring of Frank Sr. as a script reader). In return, Sylvester would give the studio the option to make any of the films he developed. If they passed, he would be free to sell the property elsewhere.

For the most part, the relationship with Paramount over the next year would be one of disappointment and frustration for the actor as project after project fizzled on the launching pad.

Things went smoothly enough at first, though there were some anxious moments at the Southern California lot when studio executives discovered Sylvester jogging around the grounds each day. For that hour, virtually no work was finished by studio secretaries, who would gather at the windows waiting for the actor to pass by. Discreetly apprised of the problem, Sylvester graciously jogged at different times each day, before or after hours whenever possible.

Almost at once, two pictures were placed on Sylvester's plate, one a starring vehicle and the other a film he was to direct.

The starring vehicle was *The Cotton Club,* the story of the Harlem nightclub that achieved fame during the twenties. The picture was appealing to Sylvester for a number of reasons. First, it had a script by Mario Puzo and was to be directed by Francis Ford Coppola, the team that had made *The Godfather.* Replete with music, dance, and gangsters, *The Cotton Club* had the potential to be the same kind of critical and commercial success. Second, there was the fee of $2 million he was offered, along with a rather unusual bonus: he would receive 25 percent of the money saved if the film came in under budget. This rather inventive ploy was conceived to discourage time-consuming arguments about the script or performances.

Calling the film "very special," Sylvester was happy to be doing it. Yet just a few weeks later he surprised Paramount by bowing out. He'd had second thoughts about the script and experienced personality problems with the film's producer, Robert Evans. The latter became so heated about losing Sylvester that he went public with a letter he sent to the actor about his withdrawal, describing the move as self-destructive, among other things. Considering how disappointing the film's performance was at the box office, Sylvester's judgment appears to have been on target.

Conversely, the picture Sylvester ended up directing for Paramount fared considerably better at the box office.

The movie was the sequel to the enormously popular *Saturday Night Fever,* the story of down-and-out Tony Manero, who lived to disco. The sequel, entitled *Staying Alive*—after one of the hit songs from the 1977 film—was a picture Paramount had long wanted to make. Initially, John Travolta wasn't sure he wanted to rehash his Tony Manero part when there were new roles to try. By the time his career went into a tailspin and he was more receptive, no one could come up with a script that was satisfactory. Says Travolta, "The first script was antidance. Tony wanted to go to block parties in Manhattan and social counseling, getting the neighborhoods together." He told the producers that that was ridiculous, that "the one thing I know the audience wants is for him to keep dancing. His appeal is as a tough guy who gets away with dancing."

Enter script doctor Sylvester, who, despite his extraordinary skills at rewriting weak screenplays, had his reservations about undertaking the movie. From his own experiences, he'd learned that making a sequel is "much scarier than doing the original. You're playing catch-up. It's like going up against your older brother."

But shortly after agreeing to work on the script in August of 1982, he found a way to continue the saga that was fresh and exciting to both himself and Travolta. The sequel is set five years after the first film, and Manero has decided to become a professional dancer. What he really becomes is a clone of the young and hungry Stallone himself, living in a shabby apartment, going to countless auditions, handing his picture to agent after agent, and finally getting a big break—in Manero's case, not *Rocky* but the Broadway musical *Satan's Alley,* in which he literally hoofs his way from hell to heaven and stardom. Sylvester had originally planned to have Manero star in a musical version of Homer's *The Odyssey* but elected to change it, he says, to something "more people would know about."

Sylvester's script was autobiographical in another, perhaps more telling way. Whereas *Rocky III* probed the pitfalls of wealth he himself had experienced, Sylvester had avoided involving the boxer in an affair; that would have been just too far out of character for the character. "Rocky is me," Sylvester agrees, "but he's more gallant than I am." However, Tony was different, and in Sylvester's rewrite he is torn between a poor girl who loves him and a rich girl who regards him as a sexual plaything. He hops from one to the other, and, while it's not exactly a one-to-one parallel to Sylvester's love life, the poor judgment Manero exhibits and the guilt he experiences clearly reflect some of what Sylvester was feeling about himself. He is circumspect when discussing that aspect of the script, but he admits, "I guess it was subliminal but it's true. I am drawing on past experience."

While Paramount was delighted to see the script problems finally solved and to have Sylvester directing the picture, they very much wanted to have him act in the film as well, as the director of *Satan's Alley.* The studio believed correctly that having Sylvester in the film would add to its box office appeal, particularly overseas, and would garner a great deal of publicity.

However, Sylvester was opposed to that idea for several reasons. For one thing, it would have been pointless for him as a career move. If the picture succeeded it would be considered Travolta's success, and if it failed it would be played up in the press as another Stallone failure; it was a no-win situation. What's more, Paramount did not give Sylvester any financial incentive. The studio was already paying $2 million for Travolta to star and $1 million to have Sylvester direct, and they didn't want to pony up the latter's rock-bottom acting rate of $2 million. *Staying Alive* eventually cost $18 million, with an additional $12 million spent on advertising and prints. Given the price tag for Travolta and Sylvester, as well as the high cost of location shooting, Paramount got away relatively cheaply for a film of this size.

His own career aside, Sylvester also didn't want to do anything that would take the spotlight from Travolta. "I'm vicariously up there with John," he said, and that was enough. Besides, if he were acting in the film he wouldn't be able to keep tight control on what was shaping up to be a very complex production, and that would put a lot of pressure on his star. "I told John that there was nothing he ever had to worry about except his acting," Sylvester says, "It's the way I always wanted to be treated, so I gave him that license to concentrate." Travolta appreciated that, describing Sylvester as a "throwback to the old days of making stars look good" and when it was all over declaring that he was "so panicked I'll never have that again that I'd like him to do *everything* for me."

However, Sylvester did appear in one scene, and it turned out to be a real crowd-pleaser. As Travolta is walking down the street, he accidentally bumps into Sylvester, who looks back and gives him a withering stare. The scene also points up the kind of unfair criticism that has dogged Sylvester. Critics raked him over the coals for imagining himself to be Alfred Hitchcock, who always made cameos in his own films; they refused to believe that Sylvester had done this to get a laugh and nothing more.

Sylvester did promise Paramount, though, that despite his absence from the screen the picture would not want for publicity. To that end, four months before shooting began he undertook a project that not only made headlines but also made a new man of John Travolta.

Having discovered that his new body had helped to give him a more positive outlook on life, Sylvester wanted to give Travolta the same outlook before the cameras rolled. Tony Manero may have been light on his feet in *Saturday Night Fever,* but he didn't have a lot on the ball. Sylvester wanted the new Tony Manero to move and think as gracefully as a gazelle.

"I've always been fascinated by body movement," says Sylvester, "which is apparent in the Rocky films." He didn't want Tony to be perfect. "He's a street animal who has this generic sense of survival, and that's what sets him apart from other dancers. He may not kick as high or jump as high, but there's a *fire* and urgency about it." Bodybuilding was his way of instilling both the physical and emotional strength in Travolta—the eye of the tiger—though in this case the training program was referred to as "the razor's edge."

At the time Sylvester started working with him, the 6-foot-tall Travolta was 20 pounds overweight and hadn't exercised in more than a year. When Sylvester informed him that he'd be working out, Travolta wasn't really concerned, naively thinking that that meant "diet, run, lose weight, and I'll look good." Sylvester's program was a rude awakening as Travolta plunged into a regimen that kept him busy for six days a week, up to fourteen hours a day.

Travolta admits that when he first learned of the breadth of the program he was "a little hesitant." He was reluctant not only because of the stress but because he loved to eat—and not the kinds of foods Sylvester had in mind. Travolta freely states that once he began walking along the razor's edge he was so desperate for food that Sylvester often ate with him to make sure he didn't cheat.

However, after five weeks on the plan (during which time Travolta had recurring dreams of "burying my face in a whole chocolate cake and eating my way through it"), the actor began to see a distinct difference in his physique. So did Sylvester, who cracked, "If John keeps it up, I'll have to fight him in *Rocky IV*." By the time he began filming, Travolta was so enthusiastic about the regimen that he raved about it to the press and went so far as to write *Staying Fit,* his

own very lucid contribution to the workout-book phenomenon. And while cynics would dub the new-model
Travolta as "Rocky Goes to Broadway," the remaking
of Travolta did, as Sylvester had predicted, get more
publicity than any other Hollywood event of 1983.

# Chapter

## Fourteen

*Staying Alive* was released in July of 1983, and while it didn't go through the roof the way the previous picture had done, it did extremely well, hitting the magic 60 percent level for sequels. What made it unpleasant for Sylvester was that the film was also the worst critical disaster of his career. The only aspect of the picture that received good notices was Travolta's body.

In defense of the critics, the picture does lack charm and emotional involvement and, in the dance sequences, tends to sweat and huff where the earlier film was sensuous and prowling. Sylvester simply didn't have the feel for dance that he had for boxing.

In Sylvester's defense, however, many critics went to the film with their hatchets sharpened because, against tradition, Paramount hadn't set up advance screenings of the picture. The studio claimed that *Staying Alive* simply wouldn't be ready in time because Sylvester had been kept from postproduction duties for two weeks by an inner-ear infection. The press, sensing that Paramount simply wanted to forestall reviews of a bad film for as long as possible, went to public showings fully intending to hate it.

Sylvester would never grow completely inured to criticism, although it had gotten easier to take since *Paradise Alley* when he received what he later summarized as "the worst reviews since Hitler." Sometimes a particular review would hurt him when it was transparently vindictive, an attack on him and not his work. He cites one in particular for *Paradise Alley* which said, "He's taken every bad habit since film began, since *Birth of a Nation*, and made it worse. . . . We could only recommend that he cut his vocal chords and stand as far away as he can in a crowd scene."

However, Sylvester's career no longer hung on reviews, and he simply didn't dwell on them the way he used to or challenge critics to fist fights as he had in the early days, even offering to pay their airfare if they lived out of town.

Yet, despite his relatively thick skin, Sylvester was somewhat bitter about the bad reviews brother Frank's music attracted. Frank had performed three of the movie's twelve songs (the Bee Gees did seven, Tommy Faragher two, and co-star Cynthia Rhodes one). Sylvester had always said that his worst fear was not for himself but for his "family not realizing their dreams or ambitions," and he was concerned that what was supposed to help Frank's career would end up being a setback. As it turned out, while Frank hasn't set the world on fire since then, his song *Far from Over* was the biggest hit from the film and helped sell millions of albums. This was a particularly impressive accomplishment given that the Bee Gees were so closely associated with the saga of Tony Manero. While Frank's sales success assuaged Sylvester somewhat, he was piqued all over again when Frank's song failed to win an Oscar nomination. *Far from Over* was a rousing, Oscar-caliber song, but a large chunk of the Hollywood community resented Sylvester's nepotism and said so by ignoring Frank.

Bad reviews aside, the studio was sufficiently satisfied with the results of *Staying Alive* to want Sylvester to go ahead with other films. He had decided at this point to stay as far from directing as possible for several years. As he described it, while he loved "the mechanics . . . the stress factor is tremendous. A director gets asked over a thousand questions a day. Also," he grins, "I don't let go easily, and they always have to drag me out of the editing room at the end of a picture. I become like this mad parent."

Paramount and Sylvester concentrated solely on finding him starring vehicles, yet what happened during the first half of 1983 was not so much a partnership as a comedy of errors. No fewer than five pictures were seriously suggested by either Sylvester or the studio, and every one of them fell prey to an often Rube Goldberg–like series of mishaps, misunderstandings, and hurt feelings.

After he'd dismissed the idea of doing any acting in

*Staying Alive,* Sylvester put forth the idea of doing a musical. It was something he'd been wanting to try, but Paramount was not exactly receptive. Sylvester was a man of many talents, but few people believed that singing was one of them. Sylvester backed off just a bit, talk shifting from an out-and-out musical to the possibility of doing a screen biography of the late Jim Morrison, the drug-hazed lead singer of the Doors; however, getting the rights to the songs and the coop- eration of the rock group's surviving members would have been a problem. Nor was a fictionalization the answer, Bette Midler having tried that with poor results in her Janis Joplin–inspired film *The Rose.* And if a real singer couldn't do it, chances were good that Sylvester would have even more problems.

Instead, in February, Paramount and Sylvester ten- tatively agreed to make a film called *Pluck the Eagle,* which would have been more in keeping with the actor's screen persona. *Pluck the Eagle* is the serio- comic tale of a bar owner who fights back after being taken to the cleaners by the IRS. (In one version of the script, he even stages a tank assault on IRS headquar- ters.) However, Sylvester eventually backed away from that one because he reportedly felt it was too similar to *Rocky.* He returned to the idea of doing some kind of musical and, in June of 1983, Paramount countered with *50/50.* In that one, Sylvester was to have played a seasoned mercenary who undertakes a big mission teamed with a novice. The sidekick would have been someone in the Eddie Murphy mold; in- deed, for a time, Murphy had tentatively agreed to do the picture. However, talks were already under way for *First Blood II: The Mission,* in which Rambo was going to be partnered with a male sidekick. Sylvester apparently felt that those two films were just too similar to make *50/50* viable. He briefly returned to the idea of making *Pluck the Eagle,* after which someone at Paramount came up with the notion of having Sylvester write, direct, and star in *The Godfather, Part III.*

That was a truly inspired idea. In terms of box-office, cassette, and TV revenues, the two *Godfather* films have been among Paramount's greatest assets. A third picture would not only make its own money but would bring in an entirely new audience which, in theory, would go out and rent or buy cassettes of the first two films.

Sylvester loved the idea, and negotiations began in earnest. The thinking was to tell the story of Michael Corleone's son, with Sylvester starring and possibly John Travolta playing his rival. At the same time, however, someone at the studio was careless and inadvertently did something that caused the project to be aborted.

Paramount had never given up the idea of making a third Godfather film with the original creative team of director Francis Ford Coppola and star Al Pacino. This desire became especially keen when, according to one of Sylvester's representatives, there was some concern that the actor would turn the mobsters into heroes, using them to clean up the corrupt police force.

Ideally, the Coppola–Pacino deal would have been the one to make. Not only could the saga then have picked up where *The Godfather, Part II* had left off, but the stylistic and artistic integrity of the series would remain intact.

So, at the same time that the Stallone negotiations were taking place, people at the studio continued talking with the original team. Certain factions seem to have felt that Coppola and Pacino might be more receptive to getting back into the harness when faced with the prospect of sitting by and watching Sylvester do the picture. These negotiations weren't formal, but they were apparently real enough so that when Sylvester learned that Coppola and Pacino were being talked to ever so obliquely and discreetly, the project came to a swift halt—this when all that had remained was to fine tune the agreement in which Sylvester was to receive $5 million dollars for his services.

The situation at Parmount was stalled, and meanwhile Sylvester was wooed by other studios. Vajna and Kassar's Carolco company was chomping at the bit to get the new John Rambo film under way, and MGM was panting for a *Rocky IV*, even though Sylvester had vowed there wouldn't be one. According to Sylvester, the first three films had said everything he'd wanted to say about the character. But Paramount was not about to give Sylvester up without a fight. They had a project that had been ready to go with actor Mickey Rourke, but he had to bow out ot make another picture. Thus, the studio showed Sylvester the script for a film that was temptingly reminiscent of *The Bodyguard*. This was the story of an East Coast police officer who heads to Southern California to track down the mobsters who killed one of his best friends.

Sylvester read the script, liked it, and, pending his own rewrite, agreed to make *Beverly Hills Cop*.

However, the rewrite would take him several months, and, as luck would have it, in the meantime there was a musical at 20th Century-Fox that needed a leading man. The studio offered it to Sylvester, along with a salary of $5 million, and he accepted the male lead in *Rhinestone*.

The history of the picture is unusual. After Dolly Parton scored a huge success for 20th Century-Fox in *Nine-to-Five*, the studio sought a new starring vehicle for the singer. What they came up with was a variation of *Pygmalion* called *Rhinestone*, in which a country singer takes a heavy-metal vocalist and turns him into a country star. Sylvester describes the character, as it was originally written, as "a blitzed-out, Black Sabbath type of punk singer who comes out wearing a cape made of razor blades." However, the project stalled over the matter of a costar. At first, an unknown was sought because Dolly was costing the studio some $4 million and an unknown would be relatively inexpensive. However, there was some concern about whether Dolly alone had much strength at the box office. After all, she'd received top support in *Nine-to-Five* from Jane Fonda and Lily Tomlin, and in her second film, *The Best Little Whorehouse in Texas*, from Burt Reynolds.

The problem was solved when Sylvester became available and joined the cast. From the studio's standpoint, the money was theoretically well spent. The teaming of two of the industry's hottest stars would generate more than their combined salaries in public-

ity. From Sylvester's standpoint, it was also a sensible
move. If the musical flopped, he had other projects as
safety nets. If it succeeded, he could do just one of
them and put the rest off while he stretched in yet
other directions.

It's important to note, however, that stretching as
an actor was not as important to Sylvester as succeeding in the stretch. He wasn't interested in trying to be a
character actor, a chameleon like Dustin Hoffman.
Unlike many stars, Sylvester is aware of his limita-
tions and has never taken a part he wasn't sure he
could pull off. His method of finding out, he says, is
simple: he reads his lines in front of a mirror, and if he
convinces himself that he's a certain character, then
he knows he can do it. If not, he wouldn't even try.

Unfotunately, successfully executing a part and being accepted in that part are two very different things,
as Sylvester was about to learn.

Loosely based on the hit song "Rhinestone Cowboy," *Rhinestone* is a comedy about a singer named
Jake (Dolly Parton) who bets sleazy nightclub owner
Freddie Ugo (Ron Leibman) that she can turn the first
jerk she meets into a country singer. Freddie agrees to
the wager, giving her two weeks to produce someone
who can win over the tough-to-please customers at his
New York–based country-western club, The Rhinestone. If she wins, he'll release her from her three-year
contract; if she loses, he adds another five years and
gets to sleep with her. They shake on it just as cab
driver Nick Martinelli (Stallone) pulls up, thus becoming her student. With his thick New York accent and
fondness for fifties rock 'n' roll, Nick is the most

unlikely country singer imaginable. However, after spending time with Jake at her father's home in the South, he masters the medium, triumphs at The Rhinestone, and also wins Jake's heart.

*Rhinestone* was shot in Memphis, New York, and Los Angeles from October of 1983 to January 1984, and there wasn't a day when the megastar teaming of Stallone and Parton wasn't being hyped somewhere in the media. Part of that was because of the appeal of the two stars, but part of it was also because of widespread expectation in the press that sparks would fly when the stars were together. After all, everyone "knew" what an egomaniac Sylvester was.

In truth, since *Rhinestone* was his first pairing with a star of equal stature, even Sylvester was worried that there might be a clash of egos. He says, "I wondered myself, 'Is this going to be possible?' because supposedly I had this reputation for being a real tyrant." However, he was pleased to find that not only didn't he and Dolly "have one argument," but she couldn't have been more cooperative. Cynics were equally surprised to find that there wasn't a romance between the two, predictions of which had run a close second to predictions of warfare on the set. Everyone involved in *Rhinestone* was simply interested in making a good movie.

What emerged from the cast and crew's high hopes and hard work was an entertaining, frequently hilarious movie. Despite Sylvester's inability to do musical comedy with the panache of Gene Kelly ("My physical persona doesn't exactly reek of 'funny, funny,'" he admits), the character he created is generally engaging. While he plays a number of scenes too broadly, especially early in the film, he shows a good sense of comic timing—which wasn't a surprise to anyone who had paid attention to the Rocky movies and *First Blood*. Rocky was always throwing out one-liners, and even at the height of the hostilities in *First Blood,* Rambo pauses to give a terrified soldier a tip on highway safety.

Sylvester insists that comedy isn't as far a reach for him as some people think. He says he has always tried to write and act in what he calls "dramedy—half drama, half comedy—because I think there's great humor in tragedy. As someone said, 'To those who think, life is a comedy; to those who feel, life is a tragedy.' If you just have heavy, heavy drama it becomes a wearing, tearing experience for an audience. As soon as you leave, the first thing to do is hail a cab and go to Bellevue to dry out. I mean, it's a brutal experience to pay $7 to discover you hate yourself, your mother, and everyone else."

In addition to Sylvester's able performance, *Rhinestone* has excellent songs written and sung by Dolly, most notably *Woke Up in Love* and *What a Heartache,* as well as her confident performance as the gritty Jake. It also possesses a smirking sense of humor overall, best showcased during a wonderful black-comedy scene in which Sylvester sings Little Richard's "Tutti-Frutti," accompanying himself on a funeral parlor organ without realizing there's a funeral in progress. This sense of humor is also reflected in several of Dolly's songs, most notably the duet *Stay Out of My Bedroom* and Sylvester's solo *Drinkin'-Stein.*

But the picture was panned mercilessly, much of the criticism being leveled at Sylvester's singing. To put it charitably, his voice is not up to that of brother Frank, despite months of voice lessons he took before and during filming. Indeed, Sylvester is so off-key that serious thought was given early in the shoot to having someone dub his voice. However, a large part of the film's appeal was presumed to be the novelty of hearing Sylvester sing, and the studio was afraid that whoever sang for the actor would let the cat out of the bag. They didn't want to suffer the same kind of embarrassment as the makers of *Flashdance,* when it was revealed that a double had done most of the dancing for Jennifer Beals. So the star alternately talked and shouted his way through the songs, occasionally pulling it off but more often falling flat on his face.

Sylvester adds that singing with Dolly at once made the problem better and worse. "It's not like I was simply singing," he says. "I was doing it with one of the greats. The day we started singing was the day Dolly won the Grammy, and that was *really* intimidating." Sylvester was so much in awe that as soon as they started singing together he promptly came down with psychosomatic laryngitis, which went away only because Dolly was "so instructive and understanding." Not only did she put him at ease, but she spent time between takes and during lunch giving him lessons of her own on the art of singing country-western.

Dolly was equally impressed with Sylvester, declaring, "Sly's brother Frank may have the better voice as far as voice tone, but I think Sly has the greater style as far as his deliverance, dramatics, and the dynamics and the expression. He has a good voice: it's rich and big, like everything else he does."

While *Rhinestone* didn't do as badly as some of Sylvester's other films, returning a respectable $12,250,000 to 20th Century-Fox, it had cost more than twice that and it ended up in the red. It also guaranteed that he wouldn't be doing anything else comedic or musical for a long time to come. He says that when the reviews came in he asked himself, "Why did I even bother?" having known before he started that he never stood a chance of pleasing the sophisticates who control public opinion.

Nor was that the only disappointment he suffered on *Rhinestone*. When the movie went before the cameras, the director was one of Sylvester's protégés, Don Zimmerman. Zimmerman had done a superlative job editing *Rocky III,* and Sylvester gave him a chance to break into directing on *Rhinestone*. Eyebrows were raised throughout Hollywood that such an important project was being handed to a novice, but Sylvester defended the move by stating, "I was a first-time director once, and *The Maltese Falcon* was the work of a first-time director; so was *Citizen Kane,* and that wasn't a shabby job." He is quite right when he says, "I think there's something about being a neophyte that's refreshing and hard to duplicate. Innovation usually comes about through blind ignorance. You say, 'Oh my God, I don't know what I'm doing so let me try something weird.' "

However, Sylvester's good intentions backfired as newcomer Zimmerman was unable to move things along as quickly as the studio wanted. Says Sylvester with a tinge of regret, "The film began to fall behind schedule. And the more it fell behind, the more the studio got panicky, and then everyone got panicky—it was like an avalanche of panic." After two weeks, there also seemed to be a growing sense that the film wasn't going to be as funny as it was supposed to be. Studio executives would watch the dailies—the film that had been shot the previous day—and they reportedly played distressingly flat.

The studio met with Sylvester, and all agreed that the best thing to do would be to bring in someone who could speed up the pace on screen and off. Bob Clark of *Porky*'s fame was hired, and while he did bring a breezier style to the picture, the loss of the talented Zimmerman was a blow to Sylvester, and not just because Zimmerman was a friend.

Because his own career has had so many ups and downs, one of the ways Sylvester stays happy is by helping others wherever possible. Thus, anytime one of his protégés goes down in flames, it's the equivalent of a personal failure. Despite the Zimmerman experience, however, Sylvester intends to continue sponsoring new talent whenever possible. As he told *The Saturday Evening Post*, "This world has become so highly competitive and overpopulated that there are a lot of people who have the motivation and method but don't have the opportunity. The real underdogs are the great musicians or actors or painters who don't have an arena or an audience for their creativity and dreams. I pity the potential world champions who never get the chance to put on the gloves." Sylvester intended to give people than chance.

Not just anyone, though. For instance, he shuns
political endorsements almost without exception,
though he does publicly approve of Ronald Reagan. "I
really do go with the man," he said in August of 1985,
shortly before presenting the president with a Rambo
poster at a Republican Party dinner in Los Angeles.
The essence of his satisfaction with Reagan is that
Sylvester believes "America should deal from
strength, and talk is a poor substitute for action." As
for other candidates, he explains, "I receive a lot of
requests from political candidates who want me to
support them, but I simply don't do it. There's no way
that I can know what a person's motives are if I don't
know them on a personal basis." Also, and perhaps
more important, Sylvester feels that it would be unfair
to those of his fans who didn't agree with him. "It
would be a breach of faith to the people if I participated in any kind of political activity—I think they
would be offended." Among the more prominent casu-
alties of Sylvester's very admirable stand are former
California Governor Jerry Brown, who asked for and
did not get Sylvester's endorsement when he ran for
the Senate in 1982.

As for one day endorsing himself for political office,
Sylvester dismisses that out of hand. Even if he
wanted to run, he says, it would be impossible. "Some
people have skeletons in their closets. I have a graveyard."

Sylvester's real sympathies have always been with
creative people and, increasingly, with boxers. He
does what he can for aspiring filmmakers and, shortly
after the release of *Rocky,* Sylvester also began invest-

ing in young fighters, hoping to develop them into championship contenders. Part of his interest was financial: a successful boxer can return a great deal of money to his sponsor. Part of it was ethical: Sylvester had become a firm believer in using his position to save boxers from unscrupulous promoters. But a large part of it was also wish fulfillment. As with Travolta and dancing, Sylvester was vicariously in the ring with each and every fighter.

The actor's first boxer was Lee Canalito, whom he'd seen on TV and subsequently hired for *Paradise Alley*. While that film was in preparation, Sylvester helped Canalito out of contractual problems he was having ("He was paying more in percentages than he could afford, and they just weren't giving him any fights") and set out to get the twenty-nine-year-old fighter some recognition.

Canalito not only introduced Sylvester to the world of boxing management but, as a favor to Sylvester, reluctantly agreed to go all-out with him in the ring, just so Sylvester could see if his *Rocky* training would allow him to trade blows with a professional. What Sylvester discovered was that he had a lot of studying to do. He dimly recalls that "after round one I didn't know my phone number; my *hair* hurt." Sylvester promptly retired from the ring, though the experience turned up in the final scene of *Rocky III*, when Apollo asks the new, improved Rocky to give him a chance to fight him again—in private.

While Canalito hasn't panned out as a champion, Sylvester did not become discouraged and has continued to invest in promising contenders, helping them

and adding "a little glamour—a little Hollywood, if
you will—to the world of boxing," even though he
admits that promoting isn't always rewarding for the
amount of time he has to put in.

Thus far, his most frustrating effort along these lines
occurred in 1983, when he felt sufficiently experienced
in the fight game to try and leap into the major leagues.
Shortly after the release of *Rocky III,* he offered to
promote (fund and stage) a fight between champion
Larry Holmes and a French contender. The fight was
to be held in France, with Sylvester introducing the
event from the ring. But that dream fell through just
shy of becoming a reality when, reportedly, he and
Holmes couldn't agree on the fighter's fee (Sylvester is
said to have offered Holmes $2 million).

While Sylvester was disappointed, he was not out of
the game by any means. In November, he bought "a
piece" of middleweight contender Mustafa Hamsho.
He now has a stable of promising boxers, and chances
are good that they will occupy more of his time and
money as the years go on. Not only does he spend a lot
of time supervising their training, but he also takes a
paternal interest in their lives, making certain that his
fighters have skills and professions to fall back on
when their fighting days are over. In fact, Sylvester is
so devoted that when John Travolta would head for the
cabaña behind Sylvester's house to use the Nautilus
equipment, he often had to wait in line behind boxers
who were either living with the Stallones or just working out.

Although *Rhinestone* was a setback, it helped to
make things just a little clearer for Sylvester. He says

it was "a bitter pill for me to swallow, but I had to say, 'Sly, that's it! You're an action-oriented person.'" Burt Young had realized that years before, but Sylvester had refused to believe him. Overhearing Sylvester tell a reporter, "I make my living with my mind. My muscles I consider merely machinery to carry my mind around," Young muttered, "The dopey bastard! This was probably his dream, to be a tough guy and a fighter. And now that he's done it, he's worried that the dream is gonna sit on him!"

Sylvester's latest failure had convinced him that this was indeed the case, and there'd be no more Nick Martinellis for a long, long time. But in their place, Sylvester would manage to achieve what only a handful of actors had ever accomplished. Like John Wayne and Errol Flynn, he was about to transcend the medium and become a hero himself. He once said, "I didn't create Rocky; Rocky created me." In an unparalleled one-two box-office punch, Rocky and Rambo both were about to apply the finishing touches to their creation.

# Chapter

## Fifteen

One reason Sylvester was now able to accept his lot in Hollywood with relative ease was, oddly enough, the experience of having worked with Dolly Parton. She'd been an entertainer longer than Sylvester, and he says he learned a great deal about public relations from her. "This woman is very sensitive, and she's really a genius because she knows more about public opinion and what people want, and their longings and perceptions, than anyone I've ever met."

Dolly is no less typecast than Sylvester, yet he saw how she accepted her lot with grace and even appreciation; it was an example of class and style which Sylvester took very much to heart. As he said after working with her, "I grew up a little," having learned from her that "acceptance is what happiness and peace of mind are all about."

Whether or not Sylvester could ever have been a nonaction film star, one of his problems has been that he doesn't always exhibit good judgment when it comes to selecting parts. To this day, he himself doesn't understand why he passed on *Romancing the Stone*, since the role of mercenary–adventurer Jack Colton would have been perfect for him. (Michael Douglas played the part in the film.) He is equally uncertain about why he turned down *Coming Home*, except that it was something of a downer, though it's clear why he passed on the role of Jesus in Martin Scorsese's proposed film version of Nikos Kazantzakis's novel *The Last Temptation of Christ* (a part Robert De Niro had already turned down). No doubt he could already hear the critics cackling, "Sylvester Stallone has finally found a part to match his ego" or "Will Sylvester rewrite this story too?"

After *Rambo: First Blood, Part II* opened, the comedy show "Not Necessarily the News" did a satiric movie trailer for *Christ II,* which hinted at what would happen if Stallone did play the part. Using a lookalike, the cable TV bit had him wrench himself from the cross, scoop up a machine gun, and fire away as the announcer said sonorously, "He's not turning the other cheek any more!"

Oddly enough, the part of Jesus wouldn't have been so far afield for Sylvester as many people in Hollywood seemed to think. When he first considered doing the picture, he did so with the vast moviegoing public in mind. He says, "There are 160 million people in this

country who subscribe to a religion in one source or
another, yet there's not one film that deals with it other
than in a negative sense. Like it's phony—like snake
oil." Christ was tempting, he says, because he's "the
number one icon . . . symbol of humanity, of
brotherhood, of love." Though Buddhists and Mos-
lems might quarrel with his generalization, he was
intrigued by the potential for such a picture to really
touch millions of filmgoers.

Then too, although it isn't common knowledge,
Sylvester himself is one of the most quietly devout
people in Hollywood, albeit not in a traditional sense.
He says, "I was raised Catholic, but I don't subscribe
to the Catholic religion. I do, however, believe in the
Creator source." That includes unshakable faith in
reincarnation (Sylvester believes that in previous lives
he was a wolf and is "quite sure I lost my head in the
French Revolution") and, for a while, interest in the
Church of the New World Unity, a religion he first
discovered when he returned to Los Angeles after
making *Victory*.

"It's very small," says Sylvester, who was introduced to the fifty-member church by his secretary. She
took him to meet Dr. Bernice Osman, who, Sylvester
raves, "gives off a lot of positive energy. When I
touched her hand, it was like grabbing onto a 9-volt
battery. There was *power* there." He says that Bernice
gave him a guidebook written by her husband Alan, a
book that has been important in helping him come to
grips with his life. "It's not a bible," says the actor,
but it "really deals with self-acceptance, self-punish-
ment, the laws of energy."

In 1982, Sylvester shared a representative passage with a reporter from *Rolling Stone:* "I ask for and accept the eternal amplification of the holy spirit and the sacred fire and the continuous control and domination of creator source over me, the God force. All my minds and bodies and the allness of my beingness . . . loving will . . . infinite father mother God. I accept the responsibility to be in divine love at all times." For the benefit of the reporter, Sylvester paused then and clarified, "What that says in a nutshell, is like, 'Shine it on.' "

Being interested in the Church of the New World Unity may not in itself have qualified Sylvester to play Jesus, but he looks back on it as "part of my education," and it showed him that he could get in touch with the theological side of the character better than most of his colleagues. He probably would have done a reverent, very commendable job, though ultimately he admits he was frightened by the character of Christ because "you'd be dealing with a very, very subjective side of people's consciousness, treading some very hallowed ground."

Even though Sylvester had regrets about his career, Hollywood was grudgingly coming to admit that he was an important part of the community. In June of 1983, he had his footprints immortalized in cement in the forecourt of Mann's Chinese Theater; this was especially important to Sylvester, who, all during the ceremony, couldn't help but think of how just eight years before he was an unknown living a few blocks from the Hollywood landmark. Almost one year later to the day, Sylvester received an even greater honor,

being recognized with a star on Hollywood Boulevard's Walk of Fame. There were other tributes, such
as winning the Showmanship award from the Publi-
cist's Guild in 1983, yet the thing that most helped
Sylvester retain his perspective during the two up-and-
down years that followed *Rocky III* was the realization
that there were worse things than to have a career
stumble now and then. It was a lesson he'd rather not
have had because it hit him where it hurt the most: at
home, involving three-year-old Seargeoh Joseph.

The needs of children have always been among
Sylvester's greatest concerns, not only because he is a
role model for so many young people but because he
himself had such an unhappy childhood. "I knew what
it was like to be an unwanted kid," he says, "an
abused kid. I know what it's like to be pounded into
the pavement." To this end, he gave the gymnastic
equipment from the Rocky films to the Devereux
Foundation in Philadelphia, and whenever possible he
has taken the time to personally answer heartfelt letters from young fans.

But nothing cuts through Sylvester's tough-guy public persona faster than a sick or needy child. Among
his most vivid memories is the morning he visited a
children's ward in the hospital where he underwent his
*Rocky II* surgery. A well-wisher had sent Sylvester a
cake with a plastic car on top, and the actor thought it
was something that the youngsters in the hospital
might enjoy more. Carrying it over to the children's
leukemia ward, he says, "I walked in and sort of
casually said, 'Hey, how's everything?' And then I

looked around and I was stunned." The first thing he saw, he says, was a mother sitting with her son, who lay shrunken and hairless in her arms. "You could just see impending death in his mother's eyes," he continues, his voice quavering. "The boy was so weak, but he touched the plastic car and managed to smile. The helplessness of her situation, the anger she must have felt . . . it just tore me apart."

Sylvester says that he went slowly around the room, shaking the hand of every child, trying as best he could to lift the spirits of these "frail little birds." It was, he says, the saddest day of his life.

Following that incident, Sylvester actively campaigned to be named as national chairperson of the United Way. He was afraid that his petition would be denied "because my background isn't exactly snow-white" (an allusion to *Party at Kitty and Studs),* but the organization was delighted, as he puts it, to have someone who "came up the hard way and who proved that it could be done." He won the honor in 1983 and spent more time than any chairperson in history stumping for money on TV and at fundraisers throughout the country. As he said at the time, "I wanted this very badly, because you can't keep taking and taking and taking and not give anything back."

However, just what the parents of sick children were feeling was dramatically and painfully underscored for Sylvester immediately after he joined the United Way.

In June of 1983, Sylvester and Sasha noticed that Seargeoh seemed unusually withdrawn for a child of his age, unwilling to communicate with others. At first, Sylvester thought the boy was simply a "silent genius," since he was drawing and writing with skill far beyond his age. Sylvester himself had spent a lot of time involved in quiet fantasies, and he presumed that Seargeoh was following in his footsteps. However, to be on the safe side, they had a doctor stop by the house and take a look at the boy. After studying Seargeoh for a while, he concluded that the boy was autistic, a psychological disorder in which a child withdraws into a noncommunicative state. As the child grows older, the muteness and inability to respond to affection or attention frequently develops into fits of self-destruction, like head banging, and even more obsessive withdrawal. Less than half of autistic children ever learn to speak.

Upon hearing the doctor's diagnosis, Sasha says, "We both broke down. Until we learned of Seargeoh's autism, I guess you could say that Sly and I were living pretty selfish lives." They had their careers and went their sometimes stormy way. Seargeoh's disorder taught them both what a real setback was. "It's like having a child who never gets out of the helpless stage," Sasha told *People* magazine.

Despite the cool, confident, almost Rambo-like face Sylvester wears in public, he is adoring and Rocky-like in private, and it was this side of him that took a beating from his son's condition. As he describes it, "To have a child in this predicament is extremely sad. It's almost like a radio station—he fades on and off of the signal." However, even in the midst of their distress, Sylvester and Sasha realized that they were relatively lucky. "A brain scan showed there was no deterioration of the brain," Sylvester told *People,* "so there is a chance that he conceivably could recover."

Over the next few years, Seargeoh did improve slowly but steadily. His parents involved him in experimental programs, such as treatment with the steroid methylprednisolone, which, while it improved the boy's speech, made him extremely hyperactive and had to be discontinued. Other medications have resulted in negligible results or similar tradeoffs, all of which Sasha sums up as "frustrating."

Fortunately, Seargeoh is considered a high-functioning autistic. He attends a special class in a Pasadena public school where, says Sasha, his "therapy is geared toward communication." This includes extracurricular trips to the store or the zoo, where the boy is encouraged to buy things or to ask to see certain animals, all in the hopes of bringing him out. And not only isn't he violent, but he can feed himself, look after his own room, and play quietly and contentedly with his toys. He has also learned to speak a few phrases, such as "Open this" or "Music, please," and Sasha says that when she showed him a videotape of *Rocky* one day, "Seargeoh cried out, 'Oh no, help, please!'" during the climactic fight.

Sylvester does his part as well. In addition to spending as much time as possible with Seargeoh, he has built a very special playground in the backyard, one he describes as "a New England environment, where Seargeoh can go outside and relate to nature and hear the flowing water. That seems to bring him out." He admits it's often painful to be with Seargeoh, since "there's no real father-and-son thing there. I have to become his playmate." More important, that also means he's had to learn to "put away your ego; you can't force him into your world. I sort of go along with whatever he's doing." These activities are, typically, drawing ("abstract things," says Sylvester) and working on puzzles. The actor admits that what's particularly rough about Seargeoh's condition is that he "has shown an extraordinary memory, but he can't *apply* what he has learned."

No matter how troubled Sylvester becomes, he remains characteristically optimistic about his son's future. Indeed, ever the fighter, he has arranged for the premieres of all his films since *Staying Alive* to be held for the benefit of autism research. This is conducted under the auspices of a fund the Stallones themselves established within the National Society for Children and Adults with Autism. Sasha works with the group on a day-to-day basis. Sylvester shows up for fundraisers, dinners, and telethons, efforts that have raised in excess of $1 million for research. Through it all, the Stallones have also not forgotten that Seargeoh's older brother requires special attention. Sasha describes Sage as feeling "like an only child, and it's lonely for him," and she compensates by having "lots of sleepovers with Sage's friends" and by going places just with him whenever possible.

As it turned out, Sage got to do more things with his mother than he ever anticipated when he became the man of the house just over two years after his brother's condition was diagnosed. Sylvester and his wife parted for good when Sasha filed for divorce on November 29, 1984. It wasn't hatred that did it or another of Sylvester's affairs. It was simply the fact that they were moving in two totally different worlds and growing further and further apart.

"All of her priorities are geared toward finding a cure for autism," says Sylvester admiringly, while for her part Sasha realized that "Sly couldn't get as involved because of his work. So I just said, 'Give me the money, and I'll take care of it.' " He did, and in short order the two of them concluded that they would both be happier and more productive if they didn't have the added pressure of trying to keep their marriage on track.

Sasha and the children moved into a house six blocks from their former Pacific Palisades home. Sylvester kept that mansion, dividing his time between it and a Malibu beach house. He was granted unlimited visitation rights and, when he is not working on a film, spends several days each week with the children.

What these personal setbacks have done is to make Sylvester realize that life is "more than sunglasses and hit movies," an acknowledgment that has helped to bring a remarkable calm to his life. Professionally, having come to grips with the fact that he'd be doing adventure pictures for the foreseeable future, Sylvester turned his attention to Paramount's *Beverly Hills Cop* early in 1984.

As originally written, the script was actually an

action comedy in which the violence was tame, almost slapstick in parts. The cop, too, had an edge of cockiness Sylvester didn't feel was entirely appropriate for his persona.

According to coproducer Don Simpson, Sylvester took the script to do what Simpson understood was simply going to be a "dialogue polish." Instead, the coproducer says he came back with a script that was considerably different, one with a "tough, Godfatherish quality."

Sylvester doesn't deny that he made some extensive alterations, although he says he thought it was clear that was his intention all along. "I felt the concept was really good," he says, "but the action was a little too sedate for me. And so I went into the film with the understanding that I would rewrite it. And I did. But frankly, it wasn't what certain factions at the studio wanted."

The big change was in the action and its loss of cartoonlike innocence. For example, the original script ended with a busy but more or less bloodless shootout at a drug smuggler's mansion. In Sylvester's version, the gunplay takes place at a warehouse with the eponymous cop behaving like a one-man S.W.A.T. team, taking out gangsters left and right. Sylvester also made his own character harder and less cheeky than written.

Paramount wasn't happy with the rewrite. Simpson says, "He did a marvelous job . . . but it wasn't comedic enough." That left the studio in an awkward position. If they made the picture Sylvester's way, it wouldn't be the relatively light entertainment they wanted to have in the marketplace for Christmas. But if they turned Sylvester down, it might well end the relationship once and for all.

Electing to make the film as originally conceived, Paramount released Sylvester from his commitment to do it and hired Eddie Murphy as his replacement. Not that the studio was entirely home free when Murphy signed aboard. The script had to be rewritten to accommodate the comedian's talents, yet at the same time Paramount had to make certain that absolutely nothing Sylvester had contributed to any of the astonishing thirty-seven drafts (with eleven different writers having taken part) ended up on the screen. Countless barrels of midnight oil were burned by both Paramount and Sylvester's representatives as they sifted through the sundry versions of the script to make certain that everything written by Sylvester was, in essence, returned to him.

Made more or less as a comedy with drama, *Beverly Hills Cop* proved to be one of the most successful films of all time—not because of clever plotting or particularly inspired dialogue, but simply because it was an ideal vehicle for Murphy's popular wise-cracking persona. Sylvester was neither bitter nor repentant, since he couldn't possibly have made the film that Murphy did any more than Murphy could have played John Rambo. Instead, he says quietly, "I believe it really worked out for the best. I'm a real believer in destiny or fate; it just wasn't meant to be, that's all. And it's a blessing because now I have a chance to write *Rocky*

*IV*, to do the rewrite on the sequel to *First Blood*, and to work on another script called *Maggie's Eyes*. I think," he concluded, "the Deity was watching out for me."

And how.

# Chapter

## Sixteen

Immediately after *First Blood* started racking up hefty returns, Vajna and Kassar were anxious to plan a series of John Rambo films. They hoped to arrange things so that, like the James Bond pictures, a Rambo adventure would be released every two years during the summer. With the collapse of Sylvester's involvement in *Beverly Hills Cop*, they got what they were after: Sylvester was free to start shooting *Rambo: First Blood, Part II*, with a third picture penciled in for production in the fall of 1986. Sylvester had his astrological charts cast—he prefers to begin pictures only when the stars give their okay—and with their blessings he agreed to the producers' schedule.

That was actually an ideal situation for Sylvester. If

he did a Rambo film biennially and a Rocky picture
every three years—he needed the extra year not only
to come up with a script but to recover from the
inevitable injuries—that would still leave time for him
to do an outside picture at least once a year. And with
these heroes to fall back on, he reasoned he could
actually take a chance and do something slightly different in those outside movies—nothing as radical as he'd
tried on *Rhinestone*, of course, but something along
the lines of what Clint Eastwood had done in *Tight-
rope*, taking what was essentially his Dirty Harry
character and giving him a few Achilles heels, just to
keep his acting muscles from atrophying.

Now known as *Rambo: First Blood, Part II*, the
second Rambo picture was budgeted at $30 million and
scripted by James Cameron (director of the action-
packed Arnold Schwarzenegger film *The Terminator*),
with half of the material rewritten by Sylvester. In the
finished composite, several years have passed since
the strife in Holidayland, and Rambo is serving out his
prison term by splitting rocks in a quarry. Along
comes Colonel Trautman (Richard Crenna) with a
proposition for the ex-soldier: the President will consider granting Rambo a pardon if he agrees to under-
take a reconnaissance mission in Vietnam, a dangerous assignment for which the one-man army is
uniquely qualified. Rambo agrees to hear the proposal
and is introduced to CIA official Murdock (Charles
Napier). The special operations head explains that the
government is anxious to prove there are no POWs
still being held by our former enemies and, to that end,
wants Rambo to go to Vietnam, surreptitiously take

pictures of an empty stockade, and rendezvous with a helicopter for extraction.

Rambo doesn't like the fact that if he does find POWs he's supposed to leave them behind, but he accepts the mission just the same. Flying from the government's Wolf Den base in Thailand and parachuting into Vietnam as "Lone Wolf," Rambo is furious when his worst fears are confirmed: the Vietnamese are, in fact, holding American prisoners. Managing to free one POW with the help of his Communist-hating guide Co Boa (Julia Nickson), Rambo keeps his rendezvous with the helicopter—only to watch helplessly as the chopper suddenly aborts the rescue and flies off. Back at the base, Trautman is furious with the turn of events and has a heated confrontation with Murdock, who reveals that the government knew there were POWs, although there weren't supposed to be any at that camp. Years before, the Vietnamese had demanded $4 billion for the release of all POWs, ransom the U.S. adamantly refused to pay. So the men were never released, though the government consistently denied that any were being held. By sending Rambo to a supposedly unoccupied camp, officials hoped to satisfiy families and veterans groups when he returned with proof that the camps were empty. Murdock tells the incredulous Trautman that now he can't allow Rambo to come back, since he has proof that the government lied.

Captured by the Vietnamese, Rambo is brutally interrogated by a Russian advisor. Surviving leeches, a dunking in a compost pit, beatings, electric shock, and torture with a red-hot knife, he eventually escapes with the help of Co Boa. Freeing the prisoners, Rambo not only demolishes the prison camp, but takes a sizable bite out of the Vietnamese and Russian armies as well. One particularly nasty assault is the result of Co Boa's being gunned down in an ambush moments after the taciturn Rambo has come as close to professing love as he is capable of doing.

Stealing a helicopter, Rambo does battle with a monstrously huge Soviet MIL MI-24 gunship, blows it out of the sky with a rocket launcher, and then uses his battered, smouldering craft to airlift the prisoners to the base in Thailand. Seething over the way he was abandoned, Rambo clobbers the pilot who aborted the rescue, machine-guns the communications center to rubble, and then makes his way to the side of the trembling special operations head. Unsheathing his hunting knife, he gives the treacherous Murdock an anxious moment when he throws the man back onto a desk and buries the blade deep into the wood, inches from Murdock's head. With it he offers up some advice: find and rescue the other POWs in Vietnam. "Find them," he growls, "or I'll find *you!*"

Outside on the airstrip, Trautman assures Rambo that, despite the devastation he's caused at the base, not only will he get his freedom but also a second Medal of Honor. The hero is unmoved, instructing him to give it to the POWs, who he says deserve it more. As Rambo leaves, Trautman asks him what he'll be doing. Rambo answers that he isn't sure, but it's clear that a man of his talents isn't going to remain idle for long . . .

Shooting on *Rambo: First Blood, Part II* was targeted to begin in September, and so, early in the summer, the producers began scouting around for a location that would make a convincing Vietnam. Sylvester had wanted to film in Hawaii, where the jungle scenes for *Raiders of the Lost Ark* had been shot. It was the least remote of all the locations put forth, and he also liked the idea of keeping the production and its money in the United States. However, the producers wanted to shoot outside the U.S. where costs would be much lower, and after looking into countless sites they narrowed the possibilities to three places: Thailand, the Philippines, and Mexico.

Of the three locales, Thailand was the one Sylvester preferred, since part of the film was set there and he's a stickler for accuracy. The filmmakers agreed, and the principals flew over to scout out locations. But they began to worry about the political instability of the region, specifically the very real possibility that their star could be kidnapped by radicals and held for ransom. Two months before the cameras were to roll, the producers scrapped several weeks of planning and started the search anew.

The Philippines was less volatile politically and geographically accurate but extremely restive in terms of climate. Francis Ford Coppola's Vietnam epic *Apocalypse Now* had filmed there and gone way over budget because of constant battering by storms. That left Mexico, where such films as *Romancing the Stone* and *Under the Volcano* had recently taken advantage of the low labor costs and lush jungle scenery. Flying down and taking a look around, the filmmakers found a suitable setting in the mountains outside Acapulco and, with Sylvester's blessings, hurriedly got to work with their own version of Vietnamization.

The principal set they built was the Vietnamese prison compound, which the filmmakers constructed on several acres of land at a cost of $200,000. It was also necessary to build a half-mile road and a bridge in order to reach the set, since the producers had chosen a site that was off the beaten track. It wouldn't have done to stage a difficult stunt or blow an expensive set to pieces, only to watch the developed film and find an inquisitive tourist or a passing 747 in the footage.

In addition to erecting the five thatched buildings that comprise the prison camp proper, the producers used the set as their base of operations, building wardrobe and makeup facilities, a cafeteria, production offices, an infirmary, and a helipad at the location. What's more, after all the construction was finished, it was necessary to spend several weeks replacing the vegetation that had been cut down or trampled under. It was a meticulous chore in that not only did the plants and vines have to be trucked in, fully grown, but they had to be woven in and out of the sets, as though the prison compound had been there for decades.

During these months before shooting, Sylvester was preoccupied with preparations of his own, expanding on the training he'd done for *First Blood*. Since Rambo uses a variety of exotic weapons in *Rambo: First Blood, Part II*—most notably a wood–fiberglass compound bow which shoots explosive arrows—Sylvester once again engaged an ex-Green Beret to instruct him in their proper use. As with Rocky, it's likely that Sylvester could actually have gone a few rounds with the Viet Cong by the time he'd completed his course; in fact, the picture would draw a great deal of favorable comment from veterans regarding the accuracy of Sylvester's tactics and the movie props as a whole. Everything from the uniforms to the pirate sampan Rambo and Co Boa hire to sail to the prison was thoroughly researched before being manufactured, and the picture was one of the first to earn the stamp of approval of Warriors, Inc., a technical consultancy firm created by veterans to advise movie producers on matters pertaining to the American military.

Sylvester also got ready by putting additional muscle on his arms and torso, making him more formidable-looking than at any point in his career. In July, he got together with Franco Columbo, the two-time Mr. Olympia, to begin his six-week program to put 10 pounds of pure muscle on his 170-pound form. Columbu told *Muscle and Fitness* magazine, "When we started, he had a 44-inch chest. At the end, his chest was almost 50 inches. And his arms went from 16½ to 18 inches."

The program was undertaken at George Pitasik's gym in Santa Monica, and it was not only thorough but expensive. When informed by Columbu what the fee would be, Sylvester cracked, "Why don't you just take my house and be done with it?" But Columbu maintains the price tag was necessary since he would have to put all his other work on the backburner. He says Sylvester "wanted to train full-out, just as if he were preparing for the Mr. Olympia contest. That meant two workouts a day, six days a week. I had to drop almost everything else in order to concentrate on getting him in the best shape of his life."

Columbu says that the actor's ambition to succeed was extraordinary. Columbu would do the exercise first, increasing his own weight and repetitions to more than Sylvester was capable of doing. That would inspire the actor to push himself to the limit. Says the trainer, "The more results he saw, the harder he trained." When they were through, Columbu reveals that Sylvester was doing curls with 70-pound dumbbells—quite a feat by any standards. Concludes Columbu, "If Sly had decided to be a bodybuilder instead of an actor, with his great proportions, his tremendous athletic ability, and his mental drive, he would certainly have ended up as one of the top physique champions."

Both Sylvester and the sets were ready for the September shoot, though the latter were not ready for long. After having shunned the Philippines, the production was ironically up-ended when Acapulco was battered by the worst hurricane to hit the area in forty years. Heavy rains caused extensive damage to the buildings, the new access road was flooded, and the bridge was entirely washed out. The production was forced to shut down for a week while everything was patched back together. Worse than the destruction itself, for a time the picture's star was lost in the storm. When the house where Sylvester was staying was threatened by an avalanche—the rocks being 16 to 17 tons apiece by Sylvester's estimation—the actor decided that it would be safer to brave the elements than to hang around under a crumbling cliff. Since the roads were all under water, Sylvester walked nine miles to the picture's production offices, causing considerable panic among the filmmakers when they called the house and couldn't contact him. Sylvester later said, "It was probably one of the most foolish things I've *ever* done, but I thought a forced march might be a great way to really get into character."

Even after the storm had passed, the danger had not. Special sentries had to be posted round the clock to watch for both mudslides and the rapid swelling of rivers.

Par for the course, the scenes which should have been the most difficult—Rambo destroying the camp with helicopter-based rockets—went as smoothly as could be. Naturally, these buildings weren't destroyed with missiles but with explosives hidden inside the structures. Staging this sequence required the special-effects team to rig more than 200 pounds of gunpowder and nearly a mile of primer cord, the destruction of each structure being covered by eight cameras running simultaneously on the ground and in the air. Some 400 automobile tires were set aflame to enhance the visuals by providing columns of choking black smoke.

Because the prison camp was something of a self-contained city, working there was like a vacation compared to some of the film's other locations, particularly the 200-foot waterfall where Rambo takes a stand against a pesky Vietnamese helicopter. Located ten miles into the jungle, the site had to be cleaned up considerably for filming. To accomplish this, a small crew first had to go in by burro—carrying, among other things, a small generator and 700 pounds of gasoline—in order to cut down trees and dynamite boulders so that helicopters could get in with more personnel and equipment.

From a filmmaking standpoint, the locations were rough but not nearly as fascinating as some of the innovative places the company used to shoot interior scenes. Since there are no movie soundstages in Acapulco, the producers received permission to convert the local Convention Center into a studio for several weeks, while a crucial sequence in which Rambo arms himself before the mission was shot in a crew member's room at the Acapulco Plaza Hotel. These may not have been the best-equipped or most glamorous places to film, but the costs were half of what they would have been on a Hollywood soundstage.

From Sylvester's point of view, filming *Rambo: First Blood, Part II* was considerably less painful than *First Blood*. Not that the shoot was tragedy-free. During a break in filming at the waterfall, special-effects technician Cliff Wenger Jr. slipped from atop the cliff, and as the crew stood helplessly by he plunged 200 feet to his death. Later, during a scene involving the stolen helicopter, disaster was avoided by the barest of margins when prop rockets on the chopper fell from the craft and crashed just a few feet from a group of actors.

However, neither Sylvester nor any of his fellow actors suffered the broken bones, cuts, or burns that had plagued them on the first Rambo film—though Julia Nickson, a veteran of several episodes of "Magnum, P.I.," had a few complaints. She cites the heat (in excess of 100 degrees), the lizards, and the tarantulas as annoying, and she also wasn't too fond of the sizzling hot shells Sylvester's machine gun kept spitting out. She was particularly worried during her death scene. The Singapore-born actress recalls, "I was lying in this pool of water and Sly was firing ahead of me. I had my eyes closed, and I kept hearing these little plops followed by a hiss. I realized all the shell casings were hitting the water around me." Though she was afraid they might hit her face and scar her, she kept her eyes shut, lay still, and hoped for the best.

While the shoot wasn't painful, that isn't to say, as Nickson implies, that it was easy. *Rambo: First Blood, Part II* was still a physically exhausting film to make, with more climbing, running, swimming, diving, ducking, and brawling than any picture Sylvester had ever done. As Richard Crenna told Sylvester after first reading the script, "You're nuts to put yourself through what you've written." But Sylvester doesn't do anything halfway, and his boundless vigor and enthusiasm moved director George Cosmatos to praise his star as "a Viking, a gladiator, a hero of the past." What's more, Sylvester had enough energy left over each day to work out on the exercise equipment he'd had shipped in from the U.S. *and* to write the script for *Rocky IV*. To him, the schedule wasn't so much workaholism as something deeper. As he explains it, "I always feel I'm being chased by Father Time. I feel I have a certain number of hours and minutes to spend on the earth, and I want to accomplish as much as I can before the final gong sounds."

Despite Sylvester's energy and the care that went into researching the weapons, sets, and props in *Rambo: First Blood, Part II,* the actor is the first to admit that the character is about as realistic as Superman. "Rambo has the skills of a thousand men crammed into one," he concedes. "Nobody could do all the things he does."

The disbelief that viewers must suspend goes beyond the demands typical of most war pictures—for example, the fact that an enemy soldier dies each time the hero shoots, yet the Vietnamese can't hit the broad side of a Huey chopper. It's also the fact that Rambo can defy gravity by jumping effortlessly from the bottom of a river onto the landing gear of a helicopter hovering several yards above the water (why didn't he do the same when the American chopper began to terminate the rescue?); it's his impossible accuracy with the bow as he effortlessly lobs explosive arrows onto a bridge, picking off an enemy truck with each shot; it's the way he manages to fire a rocket launcher through the cockpit window of his helicopter without incinerating the back of the chopper; it's his ability to withstand torture that would have made even the biblical Eleazar flinch; it's the high degree of terror he instills in the enemy, fear that causes a Russian pilot to leap from his own airborne helicopter rather than face

Rambo; it's the manner in which he casually grabs a huge snake behind the head, stares at it as if to say, "Sneak up on someone *else*," and then releases it; and it's also the way he can walk scot-free from an American military installation he's just trashed. All Patton did was slap a soldier and *his* career was ruined. Of course, Patton was a soldier and Rambo is a former soldier, which apparently makes all the difference in the world.

But the point of the film is not credibility. The job of *Rambo: First Blood, Part II* is to entertain through action à la *Raiders of the Lost Ark* (which, for the record, is even more implausible, though none of the critics complained). "Could Rambo live through all that?" Sylvester asks. "Most definitely not. But what we've done is primarily a dramatic effect which was to arouse the audience to a sense of understanding and pride in their country." This points up the film's second level, which is to fan the flames of patriotism lit in *First Blood*. During the period between the two films, America had finally begun to honor its Vietnam veterans. The implicit goal of Sylvester's film was to carry the healing process two important steps further: first, to make Rambo an Everyman and show that Americans have courage and could have won the war if they'd been given the chance; and second, as Rambo himself says when answering Trautman's question about what he wants from life, "I want what every other guy who came over here and spilled his guts wants: for our country to love us as much as we love it."

*Rambo: First Blood, Part II* would succeed on these levels beyond anyone's expectations. And in so doing it would not only enshrine Sylvester Stallone as a national treasure among the moviegoing public, but it would also make him a larger target than ever before for critical barbs.

# Chapter

## Seventeen

*Rambo: First Blood, Part II* opened in May 1985 at 2074 theaters—a record, breaking the previous high mark of 2010 theaters set in December, ironically by *Beverly Hills Cop*. And that wasn't the only record the film would break. The producers couldn't count the money fast enough; the picture raked in an incredible $32.5 million in just its first week of release. In all of film history, the only movies that have ever done better are *Return of the Jedi* and *Indiana Jones and the Temple of Doom*. By the end of two weeks, the new Rambo adventure had nearly doubled that total on its way to becoming one of the top-grossing films of the summer.

The box office story was the same around the world.

In Iceland, out of a population of 80,000, 13,984 people
saw the film in one theater during its first week. The
picture also set records everywhere from Holland
(biggest opening day in history) to El Salvador (the
same) to Mexico (likewise) to Hong Kong (ditto) to
Australia (where an incredible twenty-five house records were shattered—records that had been set, again,
by *Beverly Hills Cop*). Australia's records were
tainted, however, by a curious plague that hit the
environs of Adelaide, South Australia: Rambo lookalikes, replete with jungle greens and weapons, took to
killing animals and terrorizing picnickers. The so-
called Rambo cult thrived from May through September, after which the thrill of decapitating kangaroos
and stalking people in parks wore off.

The only other sour note in the film's overseas
openings was sounded in the United Kingdom in
August by the 30,000-member British Safety Council.
The group petitioned Parliament to ban the film, which
they described as "ninety-six minutes of mindless
violence." In their complaint, the weak-kneed group
said it was horrified "by pictures of humans blown to
pieces in close-up, and being impaled to trees by
arrows." However, the group was turned down by the
censors. As licensing committee chairperson Matthew
Adam said, the violence "was so juvenile it was laugh-
able." As with most efforts of this type, the outcry
only served to draw attention to the film, which
opened and mowed down protests and box office records alike. In fact, the film garnered so much publicity
that the advertising budget was slashed dramatically.

*Rambo: First Blood, Part II* also set another record overseas, albeit one the producers would just as soon not have to their credit: the picture was an unparalleled hit in the illegal videocassette market. Says Carolco attorney Dan Mark, "There is more illegal activity with *Rambo* than with any other picture to date," including *E.T.* and the *Star Wars* films. The producers had already spent more than $300,000 to file for trademark protection overseas, and now $1 million extra was required to police and prosecute infractors whose efforts were undermining the film's box office performance, especially in Southeast Asia and the Middle East. Before the release of the official videocassette version in January of 1986, Mark says that revenues "well into the seven figures" were siphoned off to the black market.

By fall, the picture's haul from around the world approached the quarter-billion-dollar mark—not bad considering how Sylvester had been worried he'd never have a hit without boxing gloves. Significantly, in the U.S., 37 percent of the people who saw the film went back to see it again, and 22 percent of those went back a third time, indicating a high level of identification with and/or interest in the character. By midsummer, ads for the picture were encouraging other moviegoers to do the same, proclaiming, "America's #1 movie gets more exciting each time you see it." That was encouraging news to Vajna and Kassar, who could count on a large core audience for future Rambo films. It was also a tribute to their determination. Never in movie history had an independent production company made a movie this successful. Power in Hollywood would never again dwell solely in the hands of the big studios.

What was even more interesting to market researchers was that 45 percent of the picture's total audience was female. The violence notwithstanding, women were going to the picture to see the new 1985-model Stallone, pectorals razor-scarred but gleaming. That was good news to Sylvester, since women usually make the decision about what movies to see. As long as he took off his shirt sometime during a movie, he might have more leeway than he'd thought in accepting parts.

Meanwhile, Rambo himself became as familiar a figure in the news as he was in the theaters. He cropped up on the front pages of newspapers when, just before a press conference following the release of the TWA hostages, President Reagan was overhead to say, "After seeing *Rambo* last night, boy, I know what to do the next time this happens." Rambo also appeared in countless editorial cartoons, the most famous being Bay Rigby's parody of the movie ad, showing the President heading for Nicaragua in *Ronbo: Vietnam, Part II* (complete with quotes from the critics, such as Tip O'Neill's "Oh, dear me!"). Rambo even appeared in the classified pages of the illustrious newspaper *Advertising Age,* when a company advertised for a "Rambo Account Executive . . . to blow the client's socks off."

Rambo's appeal was analyzed on the "Phil Donahue" show, poked fun at on "The Tonight Show," decried in the press by public figures such as Nebraska's governor and Medal of Honor winner Bob Kerrey, who complained that "it made [the war] look like fun," and U.S. Army Recruiting Command spokesperson Lt. Col. John F. Cullen, who didn't want his personnel putting up Rambo posters to entice young men to enlist, pointing out "the guy's an ex-convict . . . not the kind of guy we want for our poster boy." Even the screen's previous master of macho mayhem, Clint Eastwood, threw a few stones when he told *Newsweek,* "I started out [doing] the things that Stallone and some of the others are doing now. If I wanted to go out and make some dough, I could gun 'em down as good as I ever did. But I'd rather not do movies where there are 800 guys in the theater and one chick who was coerced into going by her brother." Obviously, Eastwood hadn't seen the statistics on the film's audience.

To no one's surprise, the critics tended to be extremely hostile to the movie. *The Wall Street Journal* called it "hare-brained," *The New Yorker* dismissed it as "narcissistic jingoism," and the *Washington Post* chided, "Sly's body looks fine. Now can't you come up with a workout for his soul?" Even reviewers who found the picture entertaining condemned its graphic violence. *First Blood* had had its moments of sadism, but this time Rambo really did vent his spleen, his outbursts including pinning a soldier to a tree with an arrow through the forehead, blasting another to bits with an explosive arrow, and various gruesome machine gunnings, knifings, and strangulations. *People* magazine went so far as to pan the film and to do a rather disapproving article about the high death rate, reporting that, discounting "the anonymous hordes killed in the movie's seventy-plus explosions," someone is murdered on the average of every 2.1 minutes. *People* also ran a sarcastic trivia quiz which concluded with the question, "How many international treaties does Rambo break during the movie?"

Pro or con, the opinions didn't matter. The public was smitten with the hero, and as soon as his impact became clear, licensors lined up to get a piece of the hunk. The David Morrell novelization was a bestseller for months, with nearly 1 million copies sold, and even the soundtrack album did brisk business (although Frank Stallone's truly insipid ballad from the film, "Peace in Our Life," failed to stir any radio action). Other licensors turned out everything from posters to T-shirts to water machine guns, with a newspaper comic strip and even a Saturday-morning cartoon show being put into development. However, the most spirited bidding occurred over the rights to manufacture a Rambo action doll, with Coleco and Hasbro going head to head for the privilege. Coleco emerged victorious, producing a 6-inch-tall, fully articulated figure in time for Christmas of 1985. The doll came complete with weapons and vehicles—as company spokesperson Barbara Wruck put it, "all the things that create a proper play environment."

Obviously smarting from having lost out on the character, Hasbro, which also manufactures the G.I. Joe doll, complained that while their figure is "a children's action toy, Rambo is a character from an R-rated movie." Wruck squashed those sour grapes by pointing out that, on the contrary, "the character is emerging as a new American hero, a hero that has a high degree of excitement and patriotism and a thirst for justice."

Then there were those who simply capitalized on Rambo, such as *The National Enquirer,* which ran a widely promoted contest offering $500 to the reader who looked the most like Rambo. ("Do people cheer 'It's Rambo!' when you stroll down the street? Then you're the guy we're looking for!")

All of this attention was exciting for Sylvester, not to mention financially rewarding. His earnings from the film are expected to approach the $20 million mark. But he was also caught off-guard by the political fallout—liberals shouting that he was putting stress on already strained relationships between the U.S. and the Far East, conservatives praising the way he went back and put the Cong in their place. Sylvester hadn't really expected to become what he dubbed "the Jane Fonda of the right," nor did he see himself in that light. He regarded Rambo simply as "a megaphone telling you that men who fought for their country deserve to be honored" and saw himself as once again taking up the cause of the common person, albeit with a patriotic slant. "I'm not political," he said. "I love my country." And to emphasize that point, he tried to show what is wrong with the country: "The one person who Rambo *should* kill [Murdock] he doesn't kill. He lets it live. Because you can't kill that kind of hypocritical government bureaucracy. It goes on forever."

His disclaimers aside, every pro-American comment Sylvester made reinforced his image as a super-patriot. Ironically, he'd been uttering dogma like this for years, but no one had been listening. For example, when he saw *Little Big Man* years ago, he told one interviewer that he was annoyed because they'd turned Custer's last stand into "a slanderous account of the men who died at Little Bighorn." Now the synergy between actor and role was enormous, and he, not Rambo, was the megaphone.

Fortunately, being regarded as a real-life hero wasn't objectionable to Sylvester; in many ways, he'd been zeroing in on it for years, like a moth to a flame. As he put it, "I've always wanted . . . to stand for something." Now that he had the responsibility, he took it very seriously, speaking up for the country whenever possible. Sometimes his comments did tend to be somewhat to the right of center, as when he said in *Interview* magazine that if he were in charge of a hostage situation "it would be a whole new ballgame—someone would have to atone. There has to be a consistent and forceful reaction from the American government, punitively."

For the most part, though, he stuck to generalities: "You can't squelch patriotism. The more you try, the more it becomes enflamed," and "America may have its flaws, but it's the freest country in the world. We don't have to keep our people in with walls and guns."

What's astonishing about Sylvester's elevation to the equivalent of a modern-day Patrick Henry is that he became a hero in spite of that graveyard of skeletons: his affairs, the pornographic film, the widespread reports of his widely spread ego, and his divorce. He even weathered a flurry of barbs about how, like John Wayne and Errol Flynn, he fought wars onscreen yet had been in school in Switzerland when he was of draft age. Sylvester insists that he had tried to get into the military twice but was turned down because of "something with my ears." He adds that during the war he never cared for "the streetcorner liberals who were trying to defame the footsoldiers."

It's irrelevant, really, what he did or didn't think and do then. Other actors had had their careers destroyed by innuendo, yet Sylvester was bigger than ever.

One reason, of course, is that *Rambo: First Blood, Part II* came at a time when the American public was not only desperate for heroes but low on self-respect. As Sylvester himself had realized, "Rambo triggered long-suppressed emotions. Suddenly apple pie was an important thing on the menu." The nation was being slandered abroad, its people murdered or held captive everywhere from El Salvador to Lebanon. As President Reagan had "joked," Rambo enabled us to feel better about ourselves. And when the adventure ended onscreen we turned to the man himself, listening to every word he uttered. He became a master at stating the case for the Monday-morning warriors. In Sylvester's simplified (some would say simplistic) overview, the U.S. went wrong, first, because "the only way to fight a war of that nature is by the air" and we shouldn't have put ground troops in until we'd "completely, shall we say, 'tilled the soil'"; and, second, because we were wearing kid gloves. Sylvester maintains, we should have said to the enemy, "Look, if we don't settle this in the next week, it's gonna be all-out, no holds barred. [But] the men in Vietnam weren't allowed to fight the war with any kind of concern to *win.*" America, he said, was and remains "too diplomatic . . . like a child that grew up so strong and so fast and so tall that it became self-conscious about its size" and bent down low so as not to seem like a bully.

He also took to handing out free advice on Central America which, predictably, went along similar lines: "If we're going to go into Nicaragua," he told *Interview,* "we ought to be prepared to go *all* the way. Otherwise, we're going to be constantly harassed and eventually humiliated. Again."

However, Sylvester did not give us his views on foreign policy only in interviews. In a stroke that was nothing short of commercial genius, he also gave it to us in his next film.

Ever since he'd finished *Rocky II,* Sylvester had wanted to have Rocky tackle a Russian opponent. But it never struck him as being especially viable; nasty Russians had a stereotypical flavor, and the picture would have played like a self-parody. But the Russian boycott of the Los Angeles Olympics, the shooting down of the Korean Airlines jet, and the very public oppression of dissidents changed that. The Russians really were bona fide sore sports and all-around heels. The stereotype became a cruel reality, and the time was right for Rocky to fleece the Soviet bear in *Rocky III*.

Sylvester chose to personify everything that was wrong with Russian society in Ivan Drago, the Soviet champion, a.k.a. "the Siberian Express." Through a combination of science and gymnastics, he had been biochemically toned and trained—including drugs, blood exchanges, and constant computer-designed exercise—to be the ultimate warrior who boxes his way to international fame. Meeting Apollo Creed in the ring, he kills the former champion. It remains for Rocky, the nonscientific brawler from Philadelphia, to show him what American heart can do. Alone, without the blessings of the American government, without his title, the Italian Stallion journeys to Russia. As Sylvester puts it, he goes "blindly into hell." There he wins the world title along with the hearts of the Russians who'd been cheering against him.

*Rocky IV* is a stirring, flag-waving movie which has provoked as much comment for and against it as *Rambo: First Blood, Part II*. A few critics have applauded it as a fable of sorts in which the Third World, represented by Apollo, is pounded down by the Soviets, only to be avenged by America. However, most reviewers have described the picture as shallow, inciteful nationalism, and to some degree they're right. The The initial press releases for the film pandered to anti-Soviet sentiment, stating that Rocky wasn't just fighting for personal pride any longer. "The Big Fight," said one release, symbolizes "the cataclysmic struggle of a much larger and older rivalry—of east against west, good against evil, freedom against oppression." Having Rocky carried off after the fight, holding the American flag above his battered face, did nothing to soften the impression. On the other hand, having the Russians eventually discover that Rocky (read *Americans*) wasn't such a bad guy after all drums home the real theme of Sylvester's picture; it isn't the Russian people who are bad, only the system, as personified by the state-produced Drago.

But, inflammatory or not, Sylvester was giving audiences what they wanted. The extent of this became
apparent long before the picture opened on November
27. In May, preview trailers began running in theaters,
clips that were short but dramatic. They opened with a
slow pan up the imposing figure of Drago, who is
standing in front of the Soviet flag muttering depreca-
tions about Rocky; they cut to a short clip of the
Italian Stallion working out and lacing up; and then
they showed the fighters' gloves coming together and
literally causing an explosion as a stentorian voice
intones, "Get ready for the next world war." Wherever the trailer played, people would literally leap
from their seats and shout "USA! USA!"—cries that
would continue well into the main feature. It was the
spirit of the summer Olympics all over again, but this
time those cowardly Russians couldn't stay home, and
it was obvious they were going to get whipped. "And
that," Sylvester said puckishly when told of the reaction in movie theaters, "is just a sixty-second trailer!"

The problem, of course, is that *Rocky IV* not only
acts as an emotional catharsis, but it also heightens the
negative feelings many Americans have for the Soviets
and especially for Soviet athletes. Rambo inspired the
same feelings toward the Vietnamese, but it wasn't
quite the same; we don't have to coexist with them to
the same degree that we do the Russians. It's too early
to tell whether Rockymania will translate to a demon-
strable worsening of Soviet–American relations,
though at some point it's likely that the President will
allude to Rocky as a solution to whatever problem he
may be having with the Russians.

What is clear, however, is that the picture has opened so successfully that it's cemented Sylvester's position as the movies' official spokesperson for America. How Sylvester will fare when the pendulum swings away from conservatism is anyone's guess; however, he's a clever enough filmmaker to sense trends like these and skew his common-person message accordingly.

All of this presumes that he doesn't manage to kill himself in the interim. For as much as Rocky may be delivering a different message on theater screens, it was business as usual behind the scenes, with the star taking his worst beating to date.

Sylvester directed from his own script, shooting the picture from March to July of 1985. Talia Shire, Carl Weathers, and Burt Young returned, as did young Sage Stallone (though he was billed as Rocky Krakoff to protect his privacy, whom the boxer must teach that despite their wealth and prestige there are more important values in life). These are values which, not so coincidentally, Sylvester was also trying to instill in Sage.

The only major difference in the making of the picture was Sylvester's fee, which had swelled from $10 million to $15 million.

At the age of thirty-nine, Sylvester knew he shouldn't push himself as hard as he had on *Rocky III*, but he did it anyway for the fans. As his worried mother put it, "No matter how many beatings his body takes . . . his fans love the Rocky movies, and he doesn't want to disappoint them."

His training at Pitasik's gym was reminiscent of the

sessions for *Rambo: First Blood, Part II,* though, according to Franco Columbu, Sylvester pushed even harder. Sylvester explains, "I've had more than my share of success. But I still don't feel fulfilled. Mentally, I've done a great deal. I've conquered my world. But physically, there's always another frontier. That's what's great about bodybuilding: you can never really peak."

And Sylvester was punished for his ambition.

The first indication of trouble occurred shortly after filming began. Shooting the winter training scenes on location in Wyoming, Sylvester says, "I was pulling this sled loaded with 1200 pounds of rocks through the snow, and I just felt something snap." He ignored it at the time, though his chest continued to hurt him. Then, two months later, two weeks into filming the climactic fight with 6-foot 6-inch, 240-pound Dolph Lundgren (a two-time European kickboxing heavyweight champion and one-time Australian champ), he felt terrible pains in his chest. He shouldn't have been surprised. Unlike in the previous films, where the fights were all carefully rehearsed, Sylvester says he "decided to throw choreography to the wind and really go for it," to give up "all sense of style, proportion, and distance and just revert to animal savage instinct." What he'd discovered when he first experimented with this tack was that it was much more realistic and made him feel like he was really "fighting for my life." So he went with it, and life imitated art a lot more closely than he'd have preferred.

The pains didn't strike him until he got home that night. Already weak and dizzy because he was fighting the flu, Sylvester suddenly experienced a hot pounding in his chest. When it got worse instead of better, the actor feared that he might be having a heart attack and had himself rushed to the cardiac unit of St. Paul's Hospital in Los Angeles. There Sylvester was subjected to a battery of tests and was relieved to learn that he hadn't had a coronary. He was "merely" suffering from a bruised and bleeding heart muscle. He'd strained it during the sled sequence, failed to give it enough rest by sleeping only four hours a night, and then had applied the finishing touches by standing up to Lundgren's sledgehammer blows, which had rammed his diaphragm into his heart.

Filming was suspended for ten days while Sylvester let his heart heal, and it was a time of tremendous frustration for him. After a few days he told an interviewer, "I'm already dying to lace on the leather. I've had serious injuries in all the Rocky films; this was bound to happen." However, he did admit that injuring his heart was the worst scare he'd ever had, making him realize that he was "going to have to diminish my intensity or *I'm* going to diminish." He shook his head. "I curse the film every day. Yet, again, I'd be miserable if the challenge wasn't here. If it's easy, then it isn't a victory, is it?"

But he went back to work at his usual frenetic pace and admits that that's probably how he's finally going to buy it one day, dying over a script or editing table, his last instructions to the crew scribbled hastily nearby.

The only thing that made Sylvester's recuperation tolerable during *Rocky IV* was the fact that he had more time to spend with his children and also with the new love in his life, model-turned-actress Brigitte Nielsen.

Born in Denmark in July 1963, the 6-foot-tall Gitte, as she prefers to be called, had a longstanding dream of one day meeting Sylvester. She says, "I was eleven when I saw *Rocky* for the first time," and all she could do for the rest of the day was think about Sylvester. She remembers, "We were having dinner and my father said, 'What's the matter with you?' I talked about the movie, and I said, 'I'm sure if I ever meet him, it would be something special.'" Meeting him remained her ambition for years, and it finally became a reality when she visited New York after finishing her first motion picture, playing the titular lady barbarian in *Red Sonja*.

Learning that Sylvester was staying at the ritzy Essex House, she called him for three days straight. Sylvester says that the hotel passed along her messages but that he was wary of phoning her. "There were so *many* calls," he says, "that I really began to become suspicious." By this time John Lennon had been shot, and Sylvester was more security-conscious than ever, especially since he knew of one "dangerous fanatic" who was out there looking to get him.

Meanwhile, growing desperate, Nielsen decided to write Sylvester a letter and enclose a composite photograph that showed her in four different poses. He later said of the photo, "She was in a bikini—and that's being generous. You could see her from every angle." She took a taxi over to the hotel, left the package at the desk, and went back to her room. Literally the moment she put the key in the door, the phone began to ring. Her voice was dour when she answered it.

"This is Sylvester Stallone," said the caller.

Nielsen perked at once, screaming, "How *are* you?!"

"Great," he said. "Listen, you've heard the expression 'One picture is worth a thousand words'? Well, this picture is worth a Webster's dictionary."

His fears dispelled, Sylvester promly invited her for a drink; afterwards, he asked her to join him for dinner. However, since he already had a date, he told her, "Look, just show up at the restaurant and pretend you know me for years." She did, and between the appetizer and dessert the two knew they were in love.

# Chapter

## Eighteen

The couple met in December, and by February Nielsen had moved into Sylvester's Malibu home. He welcomed her by ordering a $20,000 marble dining room table which was covered with glass—on which her portrait had been etched. A month later, he awarded her the role of Ludmilla, Drago's wife in *Rocky IV*.

While Nielsen had to endure cries of "golddigger" in the gossip columns and reportedly was not a favorite of Sylvester's mother (Jacqueline was quoted in one paper as stating, "I don't like her. She's just not good enough for Sylvester"), Sylvester was truly smitten with the woman. Calling her a "towering monument to womanhood," he says that while she is beautiful and poised, "she's the most *unvain* beautiful woman I've ever met. She's like a giant afghan, so unaffected." He insists, however, that it isn't just her beauty or modesty that won him over. "More than anything," he says, "it was her integrity, just plain integrity that got to me. She is the most charitable person I've ever come across." He added that her optimism and character provided him with something he very much needed in his life: "I don't have a great deal of personal stability in my own character, and she's much more stable."

While those pronouncements may have come as a surprise to the long-suffering Sasha, who had typed his scripts and struggled with him in the old days, they were music to Nielsen, who comprised the second half of a mutual admiration society. It wasn't just his body or good looks she admired. "I've had tall, muscular boyfriends," she says, "and small, skinny ones. That's not really what matters." What appealed to her about Sylvester was his self-assurance and a strong sense of identity. "I like to be controlled," she says, though she adds quickly, "that doesn't mean controlled like a dog." She simply likes a man who can help her take charge of her life and career.

Sylvester did that and, much to Nielsen's surprise, also took charge of her body. He put her on a strict diet and exercise program which threw her for a loop. "In Denmark," she says, "I swam. I've been riding horses for six years. I was never lazy about physical things, but I did them to have fun." With Sylvester, it's definitely not fun. "With Sylvester, it's get up early, start on the Nautilus machines. Then situps. Maybe several hours a day." She grins. "I like eight hours of sleep at night. Before, I arranged everything else around my sleep. Now, I have to fit in my sleep." She also isn't too fond of the diet he concocted for her, which she says consists of "fish, fish, fish, and sometimes rice."

But Nielsen does it because it makes Sylvester happy, and about the only thing she insisted upon in return, and which caused him minor distress, was that she refused to call him Sly. "I call him Sylvester," she says, "because it's prettier."

After *Rocky IV* wrapped in July, Sylvester asked Nielsen to become the second Mrs. Stallone. Though his own divorce from Sasha was still at least six months down the road, he said, "I'm not the type that would remain single. I like to feel free and independent, but I also like to have stability."

To mark the occasion he gave her a huge ring with a heart-shaped diamond—hearts are Nielsen's favorite shape—after which the couple went to celebrate the engagement with friends at the popular Los Angeles nightspot La Cage Aux Folles. From there, the couple promptly left for a ten-day vacation in Hawaii, spending the first part of the trip on Oahu and the second part on Kauai. While they were gone, the press was busy looking into the background of the magazine cover girl who was discovered by producer Dino de Laurentiis—and who, it seemed, had some secrets that were not revealed in any of the biographies issued by her public relations people.

Shortly after the lovers returned to Los Angeles, they were rocked by the very embarrassing revelation that Sylvester wasn't the only one of the two who was married. Reporters had discovered that Nielsen had a husband and a sixteen-month-old son back in Copenhagen, neither of whom she'd seen for months.

The husband was twenty-nine-year-old musician Kaspar Windling, who had married Nielsen just eighteen months before. Learning about his wife's engagement to Sylvester, Kaspar told journalists, "It came as a total surprise. I have spoken to her only ten times in the last year, but she never mentioned a thing. I reckon she wanted to be a star too much."

The revelation revived charges in the press (and reportedly among members of Sylvester's own family) that Nielsen was simply an opportunist who was using the superstar to enhance her own career. However, Nielsen vehemently denied these allegations, along with the more painful charges that she had abandoned her son, Julian.

"I probably shouldn't talk about my baby," she told the *New York Post,* "but I want everybody to know I'm not a bad mother who abandoned her kid. I got the movie contract and I knew I couldn't—what you say?—*schlep* Julian around. I had to make my career for *him,* too."

She added that, contrary to what everyone was saying, it hurt to be away from him, to have "missed his first steps. On the phone, it tears me apart. He's just learning 'mama,' and of course I'm not there." But she said she was filing for custody of the boy and was consoled by the fact that he was spending most of his time with her parents in Rodovre, a small town outside Copenhagen. Exhibiting a great deal of poise under pressure, she closed the book on the matter by stating that it was her fondest hope that Julian would be with her in the U.S. in time for Christmas.

The very public matter of Nielsen's marriage was an ordeal for the actress, but it proved doubly vexing for Sylvester. He hurt for her, of course, but what made it even more difficult was that it undermined his image as a born-again pillar of virtue. He was still married, she was married, and there they were living together. Middle America loved Rambo and loved Sylvester, but he was concerned that there might be a limit to how much he could press that love. However, he knew there was nothing to do but hunker down and ride out the storm.

Unfortunately, there was more bad news where that came from. Literally days after the Nielsen story broke, Sylvester was back in the headlines when *Playgirl* magazine bought color photographs from *The Italian Stallion* and ran nine pages of them in the October issue. The magazine also went with twice their normal press run, sending out 1.6 million copies. Editor Tommi Lewis stated, "This is the year of Stallone. He's every man's hero *and,* more than that, every woman's hero. We've had letters from hundreds of thousands of women wanting to see him nude." Since he'd refused the magazine's offer to pose especially for them, *The Italian Stallion* photos "are our way and our time to give it to them."

The pictures showed the trim, long-haired Sylvester rolling around naked and showering with one or more of his costars, flexing his muscles in front of a mirror, smoking, and on the final page facing the camera fully revealed. Sprinkled throughout the piece were quotes gleaned from interviews that had appeared elsewhere, such as "Sexiness is a confidence in being able to protect oneself—not just one's territory and personal effects, but one's ideology and philosophy" and "You can't put restrictions on people's libidos. It'll come out in other ways. I think half the wars in this world were fought through misdirected sexual energy, I really do."

Worse than the spread itself, newspapers around the country picked up the story, the *New York Post* actually running two of the less revealing photos on the front page. It was old news to be sure, but people who hadn't followed Sylvester's career very closely didn't know about it and were shocked by the exposé. It was another black mark on his image, and Sylvester's instinct was not to take it sitting down. But in mid-August, after meeting with his public relations people at Zarem, Inc., he decided not to become the champion of stars such as himself, rock singer Madonna, and ex–Miss America Vanessa Williams—both of whom had been haunted by nude photos taken of them early in their careers. Instead, he let the matter blow over. That stance, plus the poor quality of the pictures and the fact that Sylvester looked so young, helped to take a lot of the wind out of *Playgirl*'s coup: by the time *Rocky IV* opened, the past was forgotten and Sylvester was once again everyone's favorite hero.

Whatever happens in Sylvester's personal life, there's no question but that his career is on track and will remain so for the foreseeable future.

He is presently scheduled to make three films, all in the action-hero vein. The first is a police film, *Fair Game*, which will be followed by the oft-delayed MGM film *Stoner*. Originally conceived as a western about a white man with Indian blood who avenges a wrong done to his family, *Stoner* was changed to the story of a motorcycle cop who takes on a gang of terrorists. The reason for the change was twofold: not only did a pair of fine films, *Pale Rider* and *Silverado*, prove that the western no longer holds much box-office appeal, but Sylvester also wanted to do a movie in which he could use some of the action bits he'd come up with for *Beverly Hills Cop*. *Stoner* is slated for release during Easter of 1986.

The third film, which goes before the cameras in January for summer release, is *Over the Top*. Stirling Silliphant's script tells the story of a trucker who is estranged from his young son but wins him back after entering and winning an arm-wrestling competition in Las Vegas. Sylvester is being paid an attention-getting $12 million to act in *Over the Top*, which is money well spent as far as the Cannon Group is concerned. Having produced countless exploitation films (*The Happy Hooker Goes to Hollywood* and Lou Ferrigno's *Hercules* among them), Cannon is hoping that movies like *Over the Top* will help them achieve what Carolco did, making them an independent to be reckoned with. At the same time, having Sylvester associated with the project helped the company raise the additional $13 million needed to pay everyone else on the picture—not to mention the $250,000 in prize money offered to the winners of the First International Arm-wrestling

Championship which is being sponsored in conjunction with the film. Cannon received a hefty $20 million worth of advances from foreign exhibitors solely on the strength of Sylvester's name, making him well worth the expense. The actor is presently training with U.S. arm-wrestling champion Marvin Cohen to learn proper form as well as tricks of the trade, including, in Cohen's words, "how to leverage his body so that he can manipulate guys who weigh 300 to 400 pounds."

Following these two pictures, Sylvester is slated to get back into action as Rambo in a story that reportedly will have him rescue hostages held in a Third World country. Says producer Kassar, he hasn't decided whether it will be Afghanistan, Nicaragua, or Iran, but wherever they go a primary consideration will be the climate. "It's got to be hot so Stallone can show off his body." Not coincidentally, NBC has obtained the rights to air *Rambo: First Blood, Part II* in 1987 and will probably show it in May when *First Blood, Part III* opens. That ploy worked to everyone's benefit in May of 1985 when the network broadcast *First Blood* and not only destroyed the competition during the critical ratings sweeps period but also clearly helped to draw attention to the sequel.

And while Sylvester has insisted that *Rocky IV* is "definitely the final Rocky; after all, there's nothing left for him to fight off, except maybe body odor," United Artists (which was split from MGM shortly before *Rocky IV*) is confident there will be a *Rocky V* in 1988. Having Rocky help a fighter (his son?) into the ring for the 1988 Summer Olympics seems an appropriate scenario, with a climactic bout between Rocky and an S.O.B. of a coach from another country—perhaps Central America or Japan, depending upon the political climate at the time.

Sylvester also doesn't rule out that long-standing idea of having Rocky run for city government, "for councilman or maybe mayor," which would make a viable subplot.

Given the bad name sequels have among critics, cynics have taken to suggesting their own ideas for opponents, among them Rambo, Arnold Schwarzenegger's Commando, and Adrian. Sylvester himself has jokingly suggested E.T. However, no magazine or newspaper went quite so far in terms of crucifying the sequels as *Sports Illustrated* when they published a list of possibilities which included *Rocky X* with Marilyn Chambers ("not to be confused with *Rocky X*"), Walt Disney's *Rocky* (set underwater), *Rocky XVII, Son of Rocky* (starring Robby Benson), *Rocky XX, Mother of Rocky* (starring Shelley Winters), *Rocky XXI/Annie XIV*, and *Rocky XXII Goes to Super Bowl XXIV*.

Interestingly, Sylvester refuses to listen to ideas from outsiders regarding what Rocky should do next. He says, "You listen to 'em and then an hour later their lawyer calls and sues ya." Instead, whenever someone corners him, "I just rush off. I say, 'Got the story already, thank you very much, got the story!' "

In the meantime, Sylvester has put the wheels in motion to make his film about Edgar Allan Poe. It's significant, though, that his success with films that have happy endings has convinced him that this picture, too, must be upbeat. Though Poe in life was anything but triumphant, Sylvester says he's found a way around that. After Poe dies, Sylvester intends to cut to the poet reading "The Raven." "Even though the film's a downer," he says, "the mind shifts gears so quickly you're back in another, happier time." He likens it to how the master directors used to manipulate film audiences, such as in *Wuthering Heights*. "You see someone dying and all of a sudden a ghost would come out and they go walking hand in hand up the stairway."

Whether he actually goes through with that ending remains to be seen, particularly after he puts himself on a Poe-like diet, which he describes as "grains and cornmeal." He will eat very few vegetables ("maybe a carrot now and then"), no fish, and just a bit of meat. The grain and carbohydrates, he says, will be very good for his "mental abilities," though he agrees that the effect may be nullified if he goes ahead and becomes a "little bit" of an alcoholic to understand what Poe himself went through.

Gene Kirkwood, for one, hopes Sylvester does his Poe film. After reading the script, Kirkwood remarked, "All I can say is that it's brilliant. If he does it, I think it will nominate him [for the Oscar]." He chuckles, "Then it will be hard for him to break out of Poe."

Sylvester has also tried producing a movie. In March of 1983, he bought the rights to the life story of twenty-one-year-old Ray "Boom Boom" Mancini and turned it into a made-for-TV movie called *Heart of a Champion: The Ray Mancini Story*. Doug McKeon starred as Boom Boom, with Robert Blake as his father. Sylvester also staged the fight scenes for the picture, which aired on CBS on May 1, 1985.

And in the back of Sylvester's mind there's also a desire to return to the theater. He told *Interview* in the summer of 1985 that he's seriously considering the stage because "theater is like boxing—having the audience ringside. It's instant gratification . . . or horrification." Though *A Streetcar Named Desire* has been suggested as a likely project, Sylvester still seems reluctant to step into Marlon Brando's old T-shirt.

Whatever he ends up doing, Sylvester admits that overall he has learned to be genuinely satisfied with what he's achieved. He lives well and he consistently dresses well, his clothes being tailor-made in shades of grey, black, and white. Sylvester claims that those colors are his favorites and cover his every mood: "Black means business, white is more sublime, and gray is an arbitrary position." He also has his shoes specially made because he has bad feet from jumping and boxing so much."

And Sylvester plans to live better still by fulfilling a long-standing dream to open an art gallery. When he lived in New York, he spent a lot of time at the Museum of Modern Art, staying warm and drawing inspiration for his own paintings. He acquired a strong taste for surrealism, and later, when he had the money, he began collecting modern art, from Warhol to Kunc. He also amassed a wide selection of Romantic nine-teenth-century art, his favorite period. He confesses that once again he is living vicariously through others, those who paint and sculpt, because one artist, working alone, can be "subjective and singular," whereas he, as a filmmaker, works at "collective art—art by proxy."

So Sylvester is more content than ever these days, and whenever he loses that sense of contentment, he goes over to a well-worn photo album he displays in his home. In it are photos Sylvester took when he was starving in New York. He says, "Every six months I'd go to one of those picture machines to see how fast I was deteriorating." He has photos of himself "in a doorman's jacket I stole to keep warm," in the torn clothes and earring he wore when he worked delivering Perrier, in the shredded T-shirt he was wearing just before he went to live at the Port Authority Bus Terminal. Flipping through the pages and then looking around at the works by Monet, Chagall and others that he owns tends to snap him out of his depression.

"You've always got to look back to see the future," he says, "because success is a transitory thing, and if you forget all your lessons, you're a fool. It's so easy to develop a sense of superiority and say, 'Hey, this is never going to end.' Well, it *all* ends. *Everything* ends, so you've got to be mentally ready for it."

As it happens, Sylvester is going to the photo album less and less these days. He has finally found his niche in life and is happy with what he regards as his mission: using his position to give hope, pleasure, and assistance to others. This means continuing to lend a hand to his brother, despite the criticism he invariably receives, as well as keeping an eye on his half-sister (his mother's daughter) Toni-Ann, a New York–based model, and in general providing people everywhere with "heroes and heroines who have to pull themselves up from the depths of despair. And as they struggle and claw and finally attain their goal, the audience says, 'My God, that's the kind of person I want to be!'" And that is not an empty example; he insists that miracles do happen. "All I can say is I'm sitting here because *I* believed it could happen."

And while Sylvester acknowledges that one day his mission, even his life must end, the workaholic is already planning for the future. Next time he hopes to come back as the heavyweight boxing champion of the world—and knowing Sylvester, he probably will.

# JOAN COLLINS

## PAST IMPERFECT

The outrageously candid autobiography of the star known to over seventy million *Dynasty* fans.

As Alexis Carrington in *Dynasty*, Joan Collins has attained new heights of celebrity. It's a role that might have been created for her – a tempestuous, strong-willed and passionate woman. That is precisely who emerges in her candidly sensational biography – a 'past imperfect' that began with a privileged English childhood and the swift transition, at the age of eighteen into reigning international sex symbol. From Hollywood to Europe and back, through three broken marriages, a courageous fight to save her daughter's life, and many love affairs, Joan Collins remains beautiful, funny, talented – and very sexy.

'Sheer heaven'
*The New York Times Book Review*

'Vastly amusing reading'
*Screen International*

'Exciting and revealing'
*Publishers Weekly*